Johannes Hartl takes us on a
also answer critical questions in
intelligent and anointed at the
brilliant book that has the potential, if read with great interest
and diligently applied, to restore the awe of God in multitudes.

PHILIPP J. SCHMEROLD
Global Kingdom Mission

God Untamed is an invitation to wonder and awe. We are not
the heroes of this story. Johannes challenges us to get down
from our rickety thrones, take off our tinfoil crowns and dare
to peer at the true King.

CARLA HARDING
National Director, 24-7 Prayer

God Untamed strips away the preconceptions and misconcep-
tions of the popular myths we have come to believe about God,
revealing who he truly is in a way that honours his incredible,
powerful, awe-inspiring character. An intelligent, thought-
provoking and engaging book – read it and you will rediscover
a sense of wonder at the magnificent God we worship.

LEO BIGGER
Senior Pastor, ICF Church

God Untamed is essentially about the nature of God, it draws
upon philosophy, psychology and literature but is primarily
biblically based. An exploration of the big questions: life, death,
judgement and eternity. These weighty topics are interwoven
with narratives from life told in Hartl's usual compelling story-
telling style. He doesn't set out primarily to inform but to draw
people into worship of God who is continually being revealed.

MICHELLE MORAN
*Co-founder, Sion Community for Evangelism; Leader within
International Catholic Charismatic Renewal*

God Untamed is filled with great illustrations and amazing stories. Johannes Hartl explores some theological and philosophical ideas and questions about who God is. It is such an inspiring, uplifting and challenging read.

JAMES ALADIRAN
Founder of Prayer Storm, UK

As an author, Johannes Hartl takes a very special and different approach to his writing, and I found *God Untamed* a most interesting and thought-provoking book. It contains a lot of wisdom and stimulating ideas, and I am very happy to recommend it, particularly if you are looking to read something different but helpful.

CHARLES WHITEHEAD KSG
Chairman, International Charismatic Consultation; Former President, International Catholic Charismatic Renewal Council

This book by Johannes Hartl seeks to cut through many of the popular myths about the nature of God that seem to have crept into the thinking and understanding of many Christians and takes us back to the supernatural reality of a God who cannot be 'tamed' or 'contained' by minds that are limited by lived experience. As Hartl says about our seeking a relationship with our living God 'lip service will not get you very far' – with its constant reference back to Scripture this book challenges the reader to step back and think or rethink about their own relationship with God. If you don't want to be challenged choose not to read this book, but if you want to re-engage with an 'untamed God' it's a must read.

GEOFF POULTER
Rhema Outreach Ministries

GOD
UNTAMED

GOTT UNGEZÄHMT

Raus aus der spirituellen Komfortzone

2017
Herder

GOD
UNTAMED

JOHANNES HARTL

TRANSLATED BY FRANCIS MITCHELL
AND STEPHANIE HEALD

Muddy
Pearl

Johannes Hartl, Gott ungezähmt. Raus aus der spirituellen Komfortzone © 2017[3]
Verlag Herder GmbH, Freiburg im Breigsau.

Published in English in 2019 by
Muddy Pearl, Edinburgh, Scotland.
www.muddypearl.com
books@muddypearl.com

ISBN 978-1-910012-69-7

British Library Cataloguing in Publication Data
A catalogue record for this book is available from the British Library

Cover design by Jeff Miller
Typeset in Minion by Revo Creative Ltd, Lancaster
Printed in Great Britain by Bell & Bain Ltd, Glasgow

CONTENTS

EXODUS

FOREWORD

During 2016, under my feet I could sense the rumblings of seismic change. The world was shifting, shuddering, sliding. A historical epoch, which had felt like it had only just started, was already coming to an end.

This epoch had begun, at least symbolically, in the cool of a Berlin night as a wall of concrete was joyfully torn down and the world exhaled in relief. The cold war was over. The hovering sense of the impending doom of nuclear winter was replaced by the warm rays of a new summer. History pivoted, and now before us there was potential. A world connected by a new peaceful order, powered by human endeavour and technological wizardry. Politics rushed to the centre, becoming almost blissfully boring in comparison to the growing array of consumer goodies before us. The Internet in those heady early days seemed to be the key which could unlock utopia. Economists promised an era of unending growth. Russia dived into capitalist freedom, China opened itself to the transformation of the market, cool Britannia emerged, Europe appeared to be uniting, the United States seemed triumphant as the world's policeman. A new world was being promised, guaranteed and made secure by technology and planning. Chaos and the untamed behind us, seemingly disappearing in the rear-view mirror.

Yet this planned world was a myth. An idol – comfortable, pleasurable and reassuring, but like all idols, impotent. The next instalment in the ongoing saga of the enthronement of the human individual at the commanding heights of the world. An extension of the project of Babel, just this time with fibre-optic cables, Reality TV and discount flights to Ibiza. The promise of the freedom of the globe. However, beneath the glossy advertisements and smooth political rhetoric, a dungeon for the individual, captive to the promise that we could have it all, imprisoned by the steel bars of our never-ending desires.

The myth of the dry and comfortable globe, a playground for the individual, could only last so long. The sea, churning and charging with force would again begin to crash against our human-made sea walls. The ancient Israelites saw the sea as so much more than a giant reserve of water: it represented chaos, the unknown, that which humans cannot control, the abode of Leviathan and the chaos monsters. A surging reminder of the smallness and impotence of humans in the face of the immensity of creation and life. And the waves came crashing. September 11th – the war on terror. The global financial crisis, the return of political instability, growing inequality, the environment, Ukraine and Syria, the rise of Big Data.

No longer did the direction of the world look so assured. Fear resurfaced; anxiety became an atmosphere. Where was it all going? Chaos was back, the sea raged. Yet, the sea is part of creation. Yahweh defeats the sea in a *Chaoskampf* – triumphing over the waves, the Scriptures tell us he places limits on the sea. In the salvation scheme of God, the sea plays its role, smashing against our idols of self-sufficiency, eroding our statues of narcissism. In the Exodus, God also held back the sea, creating strategic pathways for his people to move through.

During 2016, as the waves of chaos and cultural change continued to hit, I sensed that such openings and pathways through the sea existed in this moment. As the grand myths of our planned world faltered, a search for meaning was on again, both in the world and the church. And so I walked, watched the news feed and prayed. Asking the Father to raise a new generation in his church, who could lead us through the openings in the sea. Guides, filled with the lightness of life in the Spirit, but also gifted with the philosophical and theological depth and alacrity to speak into a world starved of meaning, hungering for a God bigger than us. A God untamed by narcissus.

Across the sea, on the other side of our globe, my prayers were in the process of being answered, as Johannes Hartl was typing out the book in its original German that you now have in your hands.

Johannes would first appear on my horizon as a kind of cult author amongst members of my church. We have a number of German speakers, and one day my friend Christoph excitedly told me of this author whom his sister back in Germany had recommended, and whose book he couldn't put down. Soon my wife and others in my church, those hungry for God to move in new powerful ways, were gobbling up Johannes' books. Not long after, in what is normally called a chance encounter but which I would label a divine appointment, my wife Trudi and I found ourselves sitting behind Johannes amongst the throngs of worshippers in the Royal Albert Hall during The Leadership Conference. Incredibly, Johannes had been reading my book that morning.

Johannes is a man of great prayer, filled with the Spirit, who can communicate the most urgent and important of spiritual truths in profoundly simple ways. In this work, Johannes shows us another gift, laying out for us with great skill, passion and a storyteller's touch, a philosophical and theological argument of the need for the Western Church to reencounter the majesty and immensity of the God who cannot be tamed.

Mark Sayers
Melbourne, Australia
NOVEMBER 2019

PROLOGUE

Bursting glass, the thin panes no longer able to withstand the pressure. The howling monster we are fleeing from is catching up with us. From the dark corridor above, a crashing and splintering of windows being pushed in by the storm. Fleeing the storm once again, we run from the cold corridor into the sparse guest dormitory. The white walls are illuminated by the flickering light of bare yellow bulbs, rucksacks lying on the ground. Everything is still safe in here, but where do we lie down, when each one of the rickety iron beds is near a window? Will there be a sudden splintering in the middle of the night as shards are thrown over the beds, over our heads?

It had started with the sea looking disturbingly unsettled. Getting up before dawn, Tom and I had started praying down by the hearth. Behind us was the skete of Agia Anna, a small monastery settlement on the rocky southeast tip of the peninsula of Athos, an isolated district in northern Greece where time appears to have stood still for centuries. Only Orthodox monks live here, otherwise it is a Mediterranean wilderness. For a few days we had wandered silently in prayer. Until today, the day of our departure and this disturbing character of the sea. One can only get here via ferry; there is no land route to the Athos peninsula, or at least not a safe, freely accessible, well-known one – one that is marked on maps. But in the dim light of that early morning, the Aegean appeared very different to how I had ever seen it before. The foamy waves were whipped, row upon row, so close together and colliding so that grey rushed seething into grey. A great splash, down there far below, seemed to mark the coming of dawn. Perhaps this would prove to be a short blast of a storm that would give way to a lighter breeze with the rising sun? Doesn't the surf tend to die down with the dawn? A vain hope, quickly dashed.

This is no overnight squall. The sea itself has awakened from sleep and has raised its head, roaring. It seems to delight in ignoring our hopes of its calming. Intoxicated by its own power, the sea only seems to increase in fury against us. We are about a dozen stranded visitors, hiding from the wild weather under a small canopy – this being where the ferry should dock, although certainly not today – a French soldier and his colleague, an Italian civil engineer and a few Germans. At first, everybody adopts their own strategy of seeking reassurance: call home, call the port authority (even though only Greek is spoken here). It can all be arranged. Sure, there's a storm, but we have plans, we have return flights. We have exactly one day left to reach Thessaloniki.

Instead, the hours pass and a whole day lapses in waiting. A small pickup takes us to the main village on Athos. The narrow road winds higher and higher through the autumnal forest: steep ravines below and alongside us, and fallen trees along the way. The storm sweeps through the treetops like a carefree boy sweeping a hand through ears of wheat. I am no longer afraid of the forces of nature, not since childhood. This violence, unleashed, seems to be demanding a little attention. And it does not release us from its grip, even in Karyes at the centre of the peninsula where there are more people. Threatening clouds travel like swathes of dark smoke over a churned-up sky. The rain starts beating down and we flee into the half-ruined Russian monastery, where we are offered steaming noodles in large tin pots and a hastily prepared overnight camp. Breaking glass this evening – breaking glass to accompany the deep, sonorous, polyphonic songs of the Russian monks. And only a one-litre bottle of resinous white wine to aid a little restless sleep.

The next morning the heavens shine brightly. With joyful steps we approach the small harbour again. Again the two Frenchmen, the Italians and we Germans gather expectantly – our flight is today! The wind has eased and hope comes with the sunrise. Finally, a uniformed man explains, in broken English, that it is uncertain whether the ferry can sail today. We have to wait. And so we wait, hour after hour. The morning passes and with it the last chance to make our flights. Everywhere, mobile phones are pulled out: calls to the meteorological services for weather reports, calls to the ferry company and to the airlines. Stunned looks: the storm may be over, however, the sea is still deemed too restless, even if the waves do not seem so big anymore. We protest and feel unfairly treated. Doesn't the port authority know how important this is to us? How important it is that we keep our appointments? One has a lecture in medicine, another a crucial meeting for a large construction project. 'But I have to be in Milan tomorrow!' Or equally in Munich, Paris or Athens. Alternative routes are considered. A forestry worker gets carried away and offers to drive us, for a few hundred euros, deep into the forest near the border of the Athos area. From there you could try it on foot; however, this is not without danger as again and again hikers have been lost, deep in this inhospitable forest. Alternatively, a small boat from the other side of the island. But this, too, is not feasible, as the sea is still too restless.

The tones of voice grow angrier, the gaze of the harbour-master more and more indifferent. Maybe the sea conditions will get better. But it's already improved! Yes, but we just don't understand the sea. 'Well, if it's a question of money ...' the French soldier launches his last desperate attempt. But the port authority is incorruptible, and even if they had been corruptible: you cannot bribe the sea. Screams and tears of anger, nothing can be bought with money here, nor changed with negotiation. We have been deposited and are stuck. 'But when a God strikes me again on the wine-red sea, I will bear it ... because I have often endured many sufferings and many difficulties on the waves and in the war,' says Homer's Odysseus as he bids the nymph Calypso farewell. I have some sympathy with the Ithacan hero in his longing to finally come home. All our plans, ripped out of our hands by the storm, lie at our feet like the splinters of thin window glass. In front of us is simply the indomitable power of the sea. And we stand before her.

I have always loved the sea. The sight of all that grand vastness. There, where the dead straight line of the horizon connects the infinity of the water surface with that of the blue sky and defines it so sharply. I have always loved the ocean with its treasures, the corals and icy depths, the shady palm beaches and the millionfold glint of the dazzling sunset on the smooth waves. And since those days of the storm back on Athos, filled with a mixture of fear and hope, between perplexed waiting and sullen resignation, I now say: I love and I fear the sea. The mudflats that lure with their expanse, their patterns and their little secrets are the very mudflats in which one can fatally lose oneself. The storms, the breakers that exult in crashing into the cliffs and those in which children frolic, are also those in which one can drown. I both love and fear the sea. And because I fear it, I wonder if it is not so much that I am frightened, rather that I have respect for it. If I had not experienced it, I would not know it. The more you get to know the sea, the more you both love and fear it; he who lives on an island probably knows it best and knows most about its dangers. He is surrounded by the sea, there is no land route. His eyes constantly wander out into the boundless view and never cease to be amazed again and again. Like the call of a seagull, the fresh breeze ignites a new hope for a new journey. At the same time, he understands what he's dealing with. He will not attach too much importance to the weather report or the seaworthiness of the ship. This is because he has already seen too much of what the sea can be like. He shakes his head shrewdly and mumbles, 'Who knows, who knows …', meaning: 'best make peace with the sea, and cooperate with tides, weather and currents'. The man on the island senses that all this will never change, and yet, despite this, he loves the sea, precisely because he also fears it.

I love and fear God, as I do the sea. I am astonished by God, as I am by the sea. Early on in my life, I started with just wonder, but, like the sea, God has become greater, ever greater. Wonder is the beginning of philosophy – Plato and Aristotle knew that, long ago.[1] But it is also the beginning of prayer. Through prayer, God grows. There is more to marvel at, more to love and more to fear. You are unable to marvel at that which you are unable to fear. To have no fear is dishonest, for there are traces of something much greater than us. You cannot worship what you cannot challenge: that is the thesis of this book, anyway. And the same One whom you love from the very bottom of your heart makes you tremble. All this about God becomes obvious to the praying person, just like the fishermen of the sea. Needless to say, the islander lives with a special awareness of the sea; and in the same way, perhaps, the praying believer lives with a special awareness of God. When he talks about what he has seen, he can appear as one from an island speaking on the mainland. As if spinning a sailor's yarn. These stories, if true, are about something infinitely remote. Far away from here, where there are solid roads, weather forecasts and mobile phones. The islander, in turn, cannot take seriously the objections of those who are safely settled and warm on the mainland. Their dry houses of blessing.

The islander knows what he has to fear, he knows best: every continent is surrounded by water and every road, if you drive along it far enough, will reach the sea. You cannot avoid it. You cannot escape God: not a chance. Lay your mobile phone aside. He is incorruptible, he is real but he is not harmless, he is … untamed.

1 Plato, *Theaeteus*, 155d:
'I see, my dear Theaetetus, that Theodorus had a true insight into your nature when he said that you were a philosopher, for wonder is the feeling of a philosopher, and philosophy begins in wonder.'
Aristotle, *Metaphysics*, Book A, Chapter 2, 982b 11ff:
'For it is owing to their wonder that men both now begin and first began to philosophize; they wondered originally at the obvious difficulties, then advanced little by little and stated difficulties about the greater matters, e.g. about the phenomena of the moon and those of the sun and the stars, and about the genesis of the universe. And a man who is puzzled and wonders thinks himself ignorant … therefore since they philosophized in order to escape from ignorance, evidently they were pursuing science in order to know, and not for any utilitarian end.'

1

PHANTOM PAIN

THE PLANNED LIFE

'Sure, I'll be at the meeting next week, unless a storm prevents me.'
Not a sentence commonly heard in a Western office. Just as
outrageous a statement would be to say you can't plan your
schedule with absolute certainty a year ahead because you can't
be completely sure that you won't already have died, or that
you won't have suffered some serious mental crisis or that war
hasn't broken out.

Yet there are certain things that we just can't get away from.
Even though, throughout the history of mankind, suffering and
death are a constant, omnipresent companion, we are stunned,
amazed and astonished if it is our own life, or that of someone
close to us, that is threatened. 'How could this happen to me?'
The same incredulous surprise resonates and reverberates in
our reaction to the news of a death: 'I can't believe it. They were
only just here.'

The unplanned is never planned for in our lives.

On the one hand, that is a good thing. No one can live
with the constant consciousness, every day and every hour, of
some possible imminent misfortune. And one might well be
concerned about the mental health of anyone who *does* live
like that. Yet the underlying sense of the predictability and

reliability of life is a clear hallmark of contemporary western life. So abundantly clear that it deserves closer inspection. That a storm – just a storm on the sea – can scupper your plans just like that, without so much as a backward glance, is incomprehensible to someone used to having complete control, to having life in the palm of their hand. And the modern world provides us with a myriad of reasons to assume that our life *is* in the palm of our hands. We talk about planning our lives: what career path to pursue, when to change job, when to retire and where to go on holiday – all these are the subject of our plans and aspirations. Even whether and when to become a father or a mother is something that is calculated and worked out – that is why there is such a thing as family planning, after all.

For those things you can't plan for, there is insurance. For lightning strikes and burst water pipes. What a deceptive play on words: 'life insurance' doesn't insure life against death, but in the case of an event that you can't prevent, someone receives a pay-out, some money. Nevertheless, somehow there persists that good feeling which suggests we can live in complete security. And if something doesn't work, the doctor will be called. Or the policeman. Or the janitor. Or the lawyer or the politician. Because basically, we assume, life can be organized. If anyone asks about this more closely, they are quickly considered a pessimist or over anxious. If anyone delves behind the ostensible security of our reality, they have perhaps simply taken leave of their senses.

The most fundamental means of finding and safeguarding our place, our orientation in the world, is language: knowing the name of the disease, at least, reassures us. The diagnosis itself doesn't bring healing, but the terror does at least become something we can talk about; putting a name to it enables further information. Statistics about the probable progression of a disease can rank the incomprehensible fate of an individual in the topographically recorded terrain of what others have experienced, and therefore we can know something about it. Even if the statistics paint a dark picture, we want to know them. Because to know these numbers yourself is better than impenetrable uncertainty. Of course, they still don't bring healing. Although the weather report doesn't change the weather, at least knowing what is likely to happen makes it a little more possible to plan for that reality.

The confidence in human technology and human science in our era is high. And there is good reason for this. In recent decades, the human genome has been deciphered, the Higgs particle has been discovered and so has a remedy for the herpes virus. The world is (or so one might well believe) better understood, brighter, and people have become kinder. And there is some truth in this. The achievements of human reason should not in any way be made light of by anyone who makes use of them daily and without question. However, it is wise to know where you stand in order to know the path that you have come down, and the one ahead that you do not yet know. It is wise to be able to distinguish between one's own field of vision and the actual horizon. And it's wise to find out how far the road on which one is travelling leads, before the sea begins.

TECHNICAL REASON

What exactly happens when man orientates himself in the world? What happens when a scientist 'explores' something? Essentially two things: natural phenomena are organized and sorted, and ways of dealing with them are developed. That bright flash in the sky is called lightning and, on the grounds of measurement and observation, is arranged into the category of electrical phenomena. Then, because we know something about other electrical phenomena, we know what makes the appearance of lightning more probable. From this it can be concluded that it would make sense to install a lightning conductor on the roof of a house. This is how we orientate ourselves in the world. A look at Wikipedia gives us information that we can then work with.

The question is: what exactly do we know from reading a few Wikipedia articles? What exactly does a scientist know? What kind of knowledge is it?

This descriptive technical knowledge assembled by human-kind assigns names to phenomena and teaches us how to deal with them. It names the flash of light 'lightning' and so manages the human experience of it. It attaches a name tag to the object. But do we thereby *know* the object? Do we capture it? Can we grasp it?

Now, what do we mean by, 'Can we grasp it?' Is it not some mythical construct, whereby the light of reason pronounces the only knowable thing? Well, it is a shaft of lightning. Yes, certainly; but the human experience is more than the word, more than the scientific category, and anyone who has ever experienced a lightning strike knows something that he who has only read about it on Wikipedia will never know. Max Horkheimer, who developed the concept of 'Critical Theory', comments:

> For the young people of today, scientific knowledge alone is true because they confuse the true with the exact, and believe that the only form of reason is what I call the instrumental – and that covers all the others.[2]

Reason does not consist only of the technical, of the 'instrumental', as Horkheimer argues.

We owe it an incredible amount. But it is not everything. That which is first and foremost in human life and goes deepest, is not even touched by it. What a person is, what it means to fall in love or to feel deep pain: none of this can be entirely expressed in words or made comprehensible by scientific description.

SHADOWS OF THE ENLIGHTENMENT

European intellectual history has often been overwritten with the simple motto 'from myth to logos'. In the beginning, the Greeks believed in the Olympian gods, the Teutons believed in

2 Our translation of a quotation from an interview given my Max Horkheimer in *L'Espresso* magazine, 1969.

Wotan and the Anglo-Saxons in fairies. And yet at some point someone discovered, or at least so our history describes, that the sea is governed by tides and not by Poseidon. That the earth is round and orbits around the sun. And as for the plague, it was not so much a curse of the gods, but instead bacteria was responsible. The light of science and the sun of reason have taken the place of the half-light of superstition.

It sounds a little like the culmination of this movement, when, at the end of his inaugural lecture in Berlin in praise of reason, Hegel begins:

> But in the first place, I can ask nothing of you but to bring with you, above all, a trust in science and a trust in yourselves. The love of truth, faith in the power of the mind, is the first condition in Philosophy. Man, because he is Mind, should and must deem himself worthy of the highest; he cannot think too highly of the greatness and the power of his mind, and, with this belief, nothing will be so difficult and hard that it will not reveal itself to him. The Being of the universe, at first hidden and concealed, has no power which can offer resistance to the search for knowledge it has to lay itself open before the seeker – to set before his eyes and give for his enjoyment, its riches and its depths.[3]

In retrospect, Hegel's words sound like a rallying cry for the then young century. Few scientific revolutions have shaped the consciousness of modern man so much as the few years after Hegel, when Charles Darwin developed the theory of the origin of species: the variety, beauty and purposefulness of the entire spectrum of animal and plant life reduced to a formula of coincidence and benefit. The impact of evolutionary theory was not only related to biology. It had the impact of demythologization. Myriads of vertebrates finally had a category and a lineage assigned to them. A simple scientific

3 Georg Hegel, *Hegel's Lectures on the History of Philosophy, Vol I,* translated by E.S. Haldane (Routledge & Kegan Paul Ltd, 1955), p.xiii.

sentence brought the unmanageable chaos of multicoloured species within a common denominator. The 'closed nature of the universe' was no longer prevalent with regard to the genesis of life, and the mask was finally torn from the face of the ghost!

Unweaving the Rainbow[4] is the revealing title of a work by the evolutionary biologist and modern celebrity atheist Richard Dawkins. So it's all down to creation?! Down to the creator?! Beyond mystery?! The magic is banished, the puzzle now solved: a rainbow is nothing more than a spectrum of refracted light and all species have developed by themselves, according entirely to natural laws.

Of course, man too is a biological species. A primate – one among many – subject to the same laws. He too is just carbon. Matter under matter. One among many, no longer the centre of attention. And just as the human mind celebrates itself as the explainer of all things, it finds itself on the periphery again. The universe, it is clear at the beginning of the twentieth century, is finite but unspeakably large. There are such peculiar laws that not even fundamental categories such as space and time are final. The universe is subject to the laws of thermodynamics and is on an unstoppable path into gravitational collapse, the complete end. It's oddly arranged around man, who on the one hand wants to plan his life and explain the world, and on the other hand suddenly realizes, as cell biologist and Nobel laureate Jacques Monod reasons, that 'like a gypsy, he lives on the boundary of an alien world. A world that is deaf to his music, just as indifferent to his hopes as it is to his suffering or his crimes'.[5] Man had to 'at last wake out of his millenary dream; and in doing so, wake to his total solitude, his fundamental isolation'.[6]

But it is not only in physics and biology that man finds himself displaced from his place at the centre of things. In the year 1899, Sigmund Freud's *Interpretation of Dreams* appears,

4 Richard Dawkins, *Unweaving the Rainbow: Science, Delusion and the Appetite for Wonder* (Mariner Books, 2000).
5 Jacques Monod, *Chance and Necessity* (Alfred A Knopf, 1971), pp.172ff.
6 Ibid.

heralding the beginning of modern exploration of the human psyche. Freud's great discovery was the unconscious: man is not only – or even at first – guided by reason; rather it is dark, instinctive soul-forces that guide him. You could say that the ego, at the risk of exaggerating, is not the master of the house, but finds itself decentralized in a being that becomes a mystery to itself.[7]

And so, does the attempt to explain humankind through reason end with the explanation that reason is not the driving force of human endeavour? In fact, exactly this assumption intensifies more and more in the humanities and the theory of science. It is the power structures of discourses that direct what we call 'true' postmodern philosophy. It concludes that talking about an objective reason that can explain everything is a dangerous myth. But what takes the place of the old certainties? Does everyone make their own truth from now on?

DARK FOREBODINGS

It is as if the person who had set out to explain and expose the world is suddenly caught up in a horrible truth. It seems that only yawning emptiness replaces the old myths. From all modern science comes so much explanation, but no sense. So many sentences, but no answers to the deepest questions. Then 'Nothing' enters the stage. Nihilism, coined by Nietzsche: the 'weirdest of all guests' sits down at the table. 'The more the universe seems comprehensible the more it also seems pointless', writes American physicist Steven Weinberg.[8]

'Being thrown out' is what the philosopher Martin Heidegger calls this state of man. Thrown into a life that is puzzling to him.[9] Approaching a death that is inevitable. Faced with the fear that is invincible. Weather, disease and traffic have

---

7 This interpretation of Freud is taken from Richard Rorty, 'Freud and Moral Reflection' in *Essays on Heidegger and Others: Philosophical Papers* (Cambridge University Press, 1991).
8 Steven Weinberg, *The First Three Minutes* (Basic Books, 1993), p.154.
9 Martin Heidegger, *Being and Time*, (1927), trans, Macquarrie and Robinson (Blackwell 1962).

become predictable. We are insured against almost everything. But the consumption of psychotropic drugs for anxiety and depression doubles every few years. Never before has there been a generation in which young people have so many opportunities and have been, in relative terms, so free from the direct threat of war, illness, death, hunger and violence. So sure, this life. So free. So disenchanted.

But is this not a clue? A clue that the rational, the secured and the logical is not everything? That there is the unsayable, the shattering, the completely uncontrollable? That the depths of the world are not exhausted by scientific description? Or a longing for it, at least? In the midst of disenchantment: a yearning for the lost spell? A yearning and searching for the ... secret.

THE QUESTION OF LIFE

It must have hit him like a blow. Around the year 600BC the history of Western philosophy begins. It begins in Asia Minor and revolves around the question of what the primordial substance of everything is. Thales of Miletus taught that water is the source of everything. Obvious if you live by the sea. And yet it's like breaking a mental dam when his pupil Anaximander explains that the *Apeiron* is the source of everything. *Apeiron* – boundless – that's what Homer had already called the sea. But from the observation of a limitless horizon – at the sea – Anaximander comes to a completely different conclusion. Since all being owes its existence to another being and is limited, the beginning of all being itself must be unlimited and uncaused. And since any definition and description would again be a limitation, he concludes with logical necessity that the *Apeiron* itself must be unspeakable and unthinkable. At the beginning of European philosophy is the realization that there is the infinite. And that everything else derives its origin and value from there. That the land of limited things is boundlessly surrounded by a sea that is itself without beginning and end.[10]

If Anaximander is right, then at this point man stands before the most important question of his life. The answer to this question will affect everything else. It is the question of whether the supreme and ultimate exists, and what it is like. It is the question of God. The question about God is the most important question of human life, the most important question of intellectual history and the crucial question about man. If we were to fully realize the importance of this question, all other questions would fade in their light.

It's a question that would make most of our everyday questions look as ridiculous as a question about a dinner order on the *Titanic*. A question that is more important than the question of origin, appearance, success and money, even health and personal well-being. It is the ultimate question. The inevitable question. The question about the sea around our island. The threatening, enticing, frightening and fascinating question about God. A thousand phantom pains remind those who have forgotten. And our world is full of them.

It is time to face the sea.

10 See: Hermann Franzel, *Early Greek Poetry and Philosophy*, translated by Moses Hadas and James Willis (Harcourt, Brace, 1973).

2

LOSS OF REALITY

THINGS WE DON'T TALK ABOUT

'So what are your thoughts about death? How do you think you will die, one day? Lung cancer, or more likely a stroke?'

This would certainly be an unusual way to open a conversation when you meet a colleague on the train. Shock, disbelief: did he *really* just ask that? A question like this, in this situation, is disturbing. It comes across as wholly indiscreet. We don't talk about these things. At least not in public, not so directly and, in any case, not at this time. But it isn't only death; other topics of discussion are also taboo in public. To ask a casual acquaintance a direct question about their personal financial circumstances would be almost as offensive as asking them about their personal sexual preferences.

Now, you might perhaps shy away from broaching these questions in conversation, except between very close friends. But the issues of money and sex are otherwise highly present and visible in our culture. When it comes to other subjects, however, it is striking that it seems unusual and perhaps even indecent to steer the discussion in their direction in public. We would rather not know too much about them. They are shown only hesitantly on television and are best avoided in conversation. Here is a list of such subjects, if incomplete:

- Suffering and ageing. It is usually the young who are featured on posters and in magazines. Even those advertising nursing homes appear to be sprightly pensioners in their best years. At any rate, the ageing of our society is not reflected in the visual media. And we are less keen to hear about personal suffering than about things that are enjoyable and entertaining.
- Death. The public visibility of death has probably never been as low in any society as it is in ours today. People only die on TV. The old and the sick are isolated from the lives of the young and the healthy, in hospitals and in nursing homes. The bodies of the dead are no longer laid out, and it seems strange to think back on a time when every village and city had 'brotherhoods of good death' and the spiritual practice of contemplating death.
- Morality. For Immanuel Kant, the question of whether something is right or wrong was at the heart of the question of how we should live. Since then, much has happened. Personal opinions and values are just left standing in our society: 'I just want to put that out there, without comment.' Attitudes are progressive, cosmopolitan or reactionary; behaviour might be cunning, outrageous or selfish, but hardly ever morally right or wrong. Particularly striking is the unspoken law never to judge what is right or wrong in questions of sexuality. It seems almost offensive to admit doubts about the common-sense view that in the area of personal sexuality everything is equally right, morally – whatever two or more people choose to do with each other by mutual agreement.
- Eternity and judgment. If almost all peoples, of all cultures and all ages, lived and still live conscious of their responsibility towards a higher power, the utter absence of talk about it today in the West has to merit attention. Of course, a nebulous hope for a reunion is readily expressed at

the graveside. But the hereafter, if anything, is understood almost exclusively as a bright light at the end of a tunnel. The concept of accountability of a person to something after death (or the confrontation with negative karma or the like) seems morally insensitive and morbid.

There are, of course, ongoing discussions about all these issues. But these are conversations that all seek to allay a degree of hardness accompanying the themes. There is discussion of suffering, but then also about medicine and new possibilities of care. Behind this stands an unspoken hope: one day, science will conquer suffering. Of course we are talking about death, but in the same breath the metaphors of autumn and spring are introduced. Herman Hesse's beautiful poem about constant change and ripening in life through parting is quoted, poeticizing about entering in to the great cycle of nature.[11] So actually, death is not so much a departure, but rather merely the transformation of a form, 'reincarnation light' works even without religious signs, and already the thought of death isn't quite so painful. The question of morality is resolved into a call for tolerance. And henceforth this becomes the only commandment of morality. There may be differing points of view on everything: every person has to be understood in the context of his own background and no judgment is to be applied to anyone. Of course, if one's freedom is restricted, that is naturally bad. But as long as something feels good to all concerned, it can't possibly be wrong. And to say otherwise is just indecent.

It is interesting that it is not only in wider society that these issues are skirted around, but also that the church is even less comfortable with them. Take, for example, any *Kirchentag*.[12] Or any Catholic saint's day. Or even any Sunday service in a normal church anywhere in the West. What is talked about and what

---

11 Herman Hesse, 'Stufen' (1941).
12 The *Kirchentag* is a biennial festival of events for discussion, critical debate and networking in the arts, politics, science, business and the church in Germany. Founded as a movement of protestant lay people by Reinhold von Thadden-Trieglaff in 1949, it was intended as a faith-based open forum for democracy, human rights, ecumenism and raising awareness of discrimination.

is preached on? Having attended at least one Catholic Sunday service every week for several decades, I have never in my life – if I remember rightly – heard a sermon on sexuality. Note: this is in the Catholic Church, which is supposedly obsessed with medieval sexual morality. Never in the two thousand or so services I've been to. And I can't remember there being anything from the platform about heaven and hell or the final judgment in a church service. Nor can I remember hearing a single sermon about hell. Not a single funeral mentioning the Last Judgment – and yet only a few centuries ago, it was a central iconographic component of church ornamentation, and only a few decades ago a constant element of popular missions and frightening sermons at the end of the liturgical year.

EGO ON THE THRONE

But why are we so hesitant to speak about death and suffering? There is hardly a subject that could be more fully present in reality than these. The hesitation to openly address the question of death and eternity, and to make it a central question of life, stands in strange contrast to the omnipresence of violence, terror and death in the media. Whilst at one time grandparents prepared for the final journey surrounded by children and grandchildren, our day and age seems to compensate for the lack of personal experience of this phenomena (which concerns everyone) with a surplus of impersonal images. Mediated by the media, a thousand times already seen (yet kept at a distance), death is no longer threatening to me. The suffering that takes place elsewhere in the world, or that which carries the name of a disease and is now treated by the best possible medical care, is classified among the things known to me, and thus a little less immediate. 'One sees it in this way, another like that', is the simplest trick to keeping a direct question away from your own heart: is it right or wrong? In the context of universally demanded tolerance, this evasion excuses a lack of position of one's own, for a morality that is not ultimately binding can't be dangerous for me. And finally, a death that is just a transformation and an eternity that is just a reunion with the beloved deceased and which does not require any change from me, doesn't confront me.

Why are these issues troubling and why do we play them down? I suspect it is because they threaten our ego. In the following discussion, the 'ego' is not to be understood as the ego of the human being, but a specific form of this ego. Namely, the idea of the individual as the centre point and sovereign power of his own life. The created master of one's own life: the 'I' on the throne. It is an idea that is rarely expressed plainly, but it has two identifying features: (1) it is absolutely omnipresent and (2) it is relatively recent. Californian psychologist Jean M Twenge comes to an interesting conclusion in her comparative study between Americans of different age groups. She scours through tons of old journals, evaluates thousands of questionnaires and compares statistical data. What is the most pronounced pattern of all? It is the increase, the sudden discovery even, of the theme of 'self-awareness' or 'self-esteem' in the 1960s, and the comprehensive acceptance of this concept.[13] Twenge recognizes glaring differences between people born in the 1950s and those born later, and calls the current generation of young people, simply, 'Generation Me': the ego generation. From their year-of-68 parents, this generation have learned the importance of the search for the true self. That authority is to be questioned. That one shouldn't have to dress formally, but that it is important to be authentic and to have self-confidence. In contrast to the hippies, who still set out to find the meaning of life, this generation is a whole lot more pragmatic. Twenge collects typical statements of 'Generation

13 Jean M Twenge, *Generation Me: Why Today's Young Americans Are More Confident, Assertive, Entitled – and More Miserable Than Ever Before* (Atria Books, 2014). Twenge's theories are not undisputed. Douglas Quenqua accuses the sociologist of ignoring statistics that contradict her interpretation ('Seeing Narcissists Everywhere', *New York Times*, 5 August 2013). Twenge has defended herself against this criticism again and again, and claims that the data draws a clear picture. It can be left open whether or not to follow Twenge in her radical assertion of a 'narcissism epidemic'; but her studies certainly describe at least one aspect of the 'normal today'. Jean M Twenge and W Keith Campbell, *The Narcissism Epidemic: Living in the Age of Entitlement* (Free Press, 2009).

Me', whose worldview now affects all age groups:

- Are you worried about how to behave in a particular interaction? 'Just be yourself!'
- Addicted to alcohol or drugs, or convicted of criminal activity? What is there that is good in all this, in you? 'I have learned a lot about myself.'
- Are you worried about your performance? 'You have to believe in yourself!' (often followed by '... and then everything is possible.')
- Should you buy these new shoes for yourself, or have that body piercing done? 'Yes, express yourself!'
- Why should you end up in an unhappy relationship, persevere in your boring job or ask your mother-in-law's opinion? 'You have to be true to yourself.'
- Are you experimenting, trying out a bad habit? 'Be honest with yourself!'
- Is it unclear when the right time to marry is? 'You have to love yourself before you can love someone else.'
- Should you speak your mind? 'Yes, stand up for your opinion!'[14]

What is striking in these statements is the central role that is conferred on the personal ego: your own opinion, your own meaning, your own needs. This is not a pessimistic statement about the youth of today being more selfish or more wicked than earlier times. The selfishness, lovelessness and small-mindedness of mankind in every new age clothes itself in new garments. But those of our own era are so familiar that they are less easy to see through. The racist sentiments of the colonial era were certainly no more harmless than today's blind spots. But in our own day and age, now we no longer belong to that particular frame of mind, it is easy to recognize them as fallacy. Concern for one's well-being, however, seems quite normal today. It is, too. But it is more than that. Our time suffers from

14 Twenge, *Generation Me*, p.50.

man's orbiting around his own ego in such narrow circles that we fall into a dizzying frenzy. In a tumult of the loss of reality.

NARCISSISM THREATENED

Is it possible to have too much self-esteem? In any case, psychology has a term for it: narcissism is the name given to an excessive preoccupation with oneself, an exaggerated opinion of one's personal uniqueness, combined with a suppression of the darker side. The problem with that? A narcissistic person can increasingly no longer see and feel what it is like for others around him. He or she loses the ability to accurately assess the real situation for possible dangers, for areas where urgent action is needed. That's what I mean when I say that the ego falls from its throne into the turmoil of loss of reality.

It's not only individuals who are affected by narcissism; an entire culture can be infected by it. In her dealings with a number of students, Twenge noticed a recurring pattern of behaviour. Bad grades or answers that were clearly wrong were defended with the notion that the teacher's position was 'also just their personal opinion'. She may have an academic title and many years of experience, but that does not give her the right to claim that she knows better.[15] In fact, questioning authority is one of the basic skills on which successful coexistence in a democracy depends. The absence of this ability, and the catastrophic consequences of this absence, have a horrific testimony in the twentieth century. However, the opposite swing of the pendulum – the complete suspension of any perception that reasonable authority can still exist – goes much too far in the other direction. No longer being able to see that not every opinion is right just because a human being expresses it is not healthy self-esteem, but a loss of reality. And what reality are they losing? The one that might endanger our ego. Twenge has compared hundreds of studies on the topic and

15 Twenge, *Generation Me*, p.29.

concludes: 'Research shows that people with high self-esteem become rude, boorish, and uncooperative when criticized.'[16]

Why is it that we find the issues, discussed earlier in this chapter, uncomfortable? Because they present a direct attack on the dogma of the self-glorification of the human ego. In suffering – not the kind which can be quickly brought under control by medicine, but in the fact that there will always be suffering – one is exposed. The questions of truth and of good and evil confront the human ego with the unshakeable rock of truth, which it already suspects in the experience of the sense of justice. Namely, that man is not the legislator of the universe, but sees himself confronted by certain laws that he encounters. And because this thought is so disturbing, the question of responsibility beyond death is also troubling. The afterlife can only be seen as a farewell, as reconciliation, as hope. As something that comforts our own ego, strengthens and unites us with others. But under no circumstances is it seen as a court of law that confronts the self with something that is more relevant and important than our own ego.

Finally, death as the end of life – as the ultimate frontier – is the most complete questioning of the ego. All dreams, goals, desires, partialities, achievements and all accumulation of property, are over. And before consoling ourselves with the idea of the eternal cycle of life, remember that which we are calling 'I' is not an ethereal form of soul and reason, but the complex interaction of physical and emotional reality. Whereas a religious man believes that there is something beyond physical death, it is equally clear that what we have called the 'me' up to now is, in death, gone in its present form. And only if there is a God is there hope that that was not all there is. In an attempt to protect his own ego, and the fiction of holding his life in his hand and being the creator of that life, man protects himself from occupying himself with these issues too closely. But it is the true reality that awaits those who do not evade these things.

16 Twenge, *Generation Me*, p.65. See also John P Hewitt, *The Myth of Self Esteem (Contemporary Social Issues)* (Palgrave Macmillan, 1998).

THE GOSPEL OF BEING NICE

One of the less encouraging results of Twenge's research is what she writes about the Christian churches. One would expect the church above all to have a counter-response to narcissism ready. Twenge's observations certainly relate more to the US and more to the evangelical scene, but parallels are easy to find. She identifies exactly those same trends in the churches as in the narcissistic society of 'Generation Me'. Based on the analysis of book titles, seminar topics and well-known speakers, she concludes: the Christian churches preach exactly the same glorification of the ego, but with devout vocabulary. Christianity is about personal development, the discovery of God-given potential. 'You are something special', is the message. True, 'because God loves you', but with the emphasis on the ego. These observations coincide with my own continental European, predominantly large-church, experience. Although nowhere is the egoism or narcissism of the individual preached, rather the contrary; it is the collective narcissism of man. It's about charity. About mindfulness. About help. Solidarity. And, therefore, about not judging. About peace. About human rights, because God 'believes in man'. The value of the family. Sunday school is about good friends this Sunday. The *Kirchentag* platform deals with the structures of global injustice in the banking business. The instruction of committed members of the parish pastorate is all about non-violent communication, and spirituality for Christian publishers is about the way to inner peace. All these are certainly worthwhile topics! But it is striking: they all revolve around people. They do not always draw their meaning directly from the conviction that they themselves are the most important thing. But humankind, that is the most important thing. The human being is the centre of attention.

SELFIE CHURCH

To lose the ability to recognize authority is to lose one's grip on reality. Someone who calls Wagner, Goethe, Michelangelo or Bach incompetent bunglers is not expressing a personal aesthetic opinion, but rather betraying their own lack of aesthetic perception. Whether it appeals to them personally is not the question; but no one who has really engaged with music will come to the conclusion that Bach composed badly or that his works are qualitatively indistinguishable from a hit single. Not to recognize the value of a fugue simply testifies to a lack of musical education. It may not be immediately clear to everyone why Goethe's *Faust* is greater art than a cheap novel from the station kiosk, and some might prefer the latter. But no one would come to that assessment after seriously engaging with literature.

In the course of anti-authoritarian education, individuals should be empowered to make their own decisions and not just to follow commands. This is an understandable, perhaps even a necessary response to a repressive education system, one that made the principle of totalitarian leadership seem an obvious form of government. The rejection of all authority, however, quickly proved to be as much of a wrong path in educational theory, even though its negative consequences might be significantly less visible. A parallel emergence of anti-authoritarian education and modern hype about 'self-esteem' also took place in Christian theology and ecclesiastical practice as a turning back towards mankind. Pastoral practice and liturgy that accommodate people; services that meet visitors at a low threshold. A church that is there for the people. A theology that understands itself as anthropology. Understandable demands with many good aspects, which, however, can have disastrous consequences if they become self-fulfilling.

A tourist stands in front of the Grand Canyon and takes photographs. He does not photograph the Grand Canyon, but ... himself. In this age of selfie-sticks, the monuments of architecture, the works of art in museums and the most breath taking of natural spectacles become just a backdrop for ... myself. The selfie flood or selfie frenzy can be considered with an indulgent smile. Of course you want to show where you have been. But the lack of astonishment at this new custom shows how normal the subtle attitude behind it has already become. Is the Grand Canyon only meaningful when it forms the background to my image? Is that photo only important because I appear in it?

Members of a congregation talk to one another as they leave the church. The choir sang beautifully. The pastor's sermon was boring. The children did get a bit too loud. The benches were uncomfortable and the auditorium too cold. The song at the end was difficult to understand. But the organ was very well played. And so charming that the priest shook everyone's hand on the way out. Overall, we did get something out of it.

What is striking about this little conversation? It revolves solely around what *someone* liked about it, on what appealed to *them*. Or to the other individuals. Indeed, it is clear that the church service is about offering something to people; that is the silent assumption. And in this middle-class parish, churches differ little from the hip, young independent churches in the city centre. Church as a service. Faith as help in everyday life. As a resource in a stressful life, as an anchor in difficult times, as an ornament at weddings and funerals, as an occasion to reflect on burnout. And even if, ironically speaking, you already have well-behaved children, a car, life insurance and orthopaedic shoe insoles, the only thing missing is a little religion. A little bit of religion to comprehensively empower, comfort and inspire … the ego.

THE SELL-OUT OF THE SANCTIFIED

A church that has lost a sense of what she is there for becomes infected by the floundering loss of reality by society itself. The church tends to become infected with the spiritual diseases of its time. Like the Western Empire, the medieval church was prone to reliance on military force. The church of Early Modern times relied on the power of money, like the aspiring citizens of early mercantilism. The church of the eighteenth century was susceptible to the deism of the Enlightenment; the church of the nineteenth and early twentieth centuries to racism, and the church of today to the cult of the ego. Yet a student who, having learned that authority is to be questioned, who no longer recognizes the difference between his opinion and that of a professor, is suffering from a disturbance of perception. And a church in which there is no longer a sense of the sacred resembles, in disturbingly precise detail, the culture of their time. Things are lost, dramatically, when the creature forgets that it is a creature and not the Creator. When it loses the sense of the last and highest majesty. What happens when we lose the sense of the sublime – the sacred? All value judgments, all ethics and all morality of man, but also all art, beauty and all sense are based on the basic ability to recognize value in something.

OBJECTIVELY SUBLIME

People have different intuitions about whether there is an 'other', something beyond human knowledge and experience. Whether what they suddenly sense in the lonely small hours as something foreboding, is actually merely a deception of the eye, a trick of the mind or shaft of light from an open door. It cannot be denied, however, that many people experience what one might call 'the absolute'. The young Alexander Solzhenitsyn joins the Red Army as a confirmed materialist. There is no God. What is law and what is wrong, that is something determined by man. In the case of communism: the revolutionary proletariat. As a soldier in the last days of the war, he witnesses the mass rape of German women. In his poetry collection *Prussian Nights* he tells of a terrible scene in Neidenburg, that is to change his thinking forever.

Twenty-two Horingstrasse.
It's not been burned, just looted, rifled.
A moaning, by the walls half muffled:
The mother's wounded, still alive.

The little daughter's on the mattress,
Dead. How many had been on it?
A platoon, a company perhaps?
A girl's been turned into a woman,
A woman turned into a corpse.
It's all come down to simple phrases:
Do not forget! Do not forgive!
Blood for blood! A tooth for a tooth!
The mother begs, 'Tote mich Soldat!'
Her eyes are hazy and bloodshot.
The dark's upon her. She can't see.
Am I one of theirs? ... [17]

The brutal sexual violence and the murder of defenceless women causes Solzhenitsyn's worldview to falter. He encounters an unfamiliar emotion in himself. With absolute certainty he knows that these rapes are wrong. Regardless of nationality and the events of war, the young soldier (despite his diametrically opposed standpoint) encounters an irrefutable value judgment: this act is, in every context, evil. It is evil, no matter what you call it. A person's conscience can be compliant when it comes to apologizing for one's own mistakes. When it comes to an injustice of which one becomes a witness, something rears up inside and screams: No! One who knows that someone else is a murderer, because one has seen it, cannot possibly be silent on the condemnation of another. At least not without having to combat a resistance within themselves. That a court may have passed judgment does not change the facts. And if everyone else says otherwise, it would still be wrong. Anyone who sees a child being tortured does not have to first study the law of that country before concluding that it is wrong.

The precise question of what is regarded as wrong is not the main issue here. This example could be used to show that different people judge differently between good and evil

---

17 Alexander Solzhenitsyn, *Prussian Nights*, translated by Robert Conquest (Harper Collins, 1977).

(although there would probably be an amazing amount of agreement even between people of different cultures). But no matter what is to be defined as wrong: the feeling of injustice itself confronts man as something absolute. Even those who are convinced that all moral values and laws are dependent on the specific cultural context will be unlikely to arrive at the conclusion that their own judgment of what is just and what is unfair is merely an expression of their own personal feelings.

In any case, that person will at least give up this position when they themselves are the victim. At the very least, if he himself is wrongfully imprisoned, he would call this process unfair and not merely an expression of another cultural mould.

No matter what exactly is considered wrong, the injustice itself is based on the perception of the violation of something. The substantive detail of the 'law' that is being violated may not be clear to you, but it feels as if there is something wrong. Let us now choose an example which may not appear to be entirely obvious. Whenever it comes to dealing with people, the objection is raised that perhaps our sense of injustice is nothing more than learned interaction with one another, which would have made it easier for the more highly developed primates to live in a herd.

The example is this: at the edge of a village stands a mighty old lime tree. It is probably a thousand years old. Its wide crown of branches extends to twenty metres across. Its trunk has survived crusades, epidemics and the coming and going of kingdoms as well as hundreds of winters. A homeowner nearby has bought a new chainsaw. He wants to try it out. He sees the lime tree, sees that it does not seem to be standing on anybody's property and does not seem to fulfil any special purpose, and begins to cut it down. After a little work, the old giant is felled and a pale stump rises from the ground where once the ancient lime tree stood.

Is it understandable why the homeowner chose this lime tree for the test run of his new saw? Is this behaviour justified by reference to the free will of the perpetrator? Where does the value judgment come from, that this behaviour might be bad? Or that the evaluation of such an act cannot be reasonably discussed? Let's say that a debating partner defends the opinion that both actions are morally irreproachable: would we even acknowledge this opinion as an opinion? Or would we not rather say, 'How can you even say that? Do you not see what a majestic tree it was?' We would barely argue with someone who disagrees here. How do you convince someone for whom a tree is just a piece of wood? One can only appeal to him to open his eyes. So see what is really here. To see ... but to see what?

To see the value and dignity of an old tree. Or its beauty. The grandeur of such an old tree. No matter what word you choose, it should be something that expresses that it's just not okay to take hold of it lightly. It is precisely this feeling which underlies moral judgments. The ineradicable human intuition that trees are not just matter. But also that things, living beings and persons should have dignity. That human life would not be imaginable if it were otherwise. The value and dignity of the lime tree is not limited to a function for a human being. The one who discovers in himself the sense of justice knows at the same moment that it is not a mere matter of personal taste. He does not exactly say that he personally would suggest trying the chainsaw on a log, because he finds it prettier that way. No, he says: it is really wrong to cut this tree down. Everything in him resists the idea of the splintering treetop. This is not just about preference. He says that it is really wrong, because there is a real value. That there is dignity. And that there is something sublime.

THE LOST MIDDLE

Now, there are degrees of sublimity. Not everything carries the same weight. And here again, any attempt at an objective ordering of the value of things and living beings according to the level of their sublimity would soon be shown to be a nonsensical exercise. Who could begin to measure that? But that there are gradations is obvious. Few would argue that it is always disgraceful to cut down a tree. But a particularly beautiful, an especially old one or one of a rare species, or perhaps one that is just special for some frivolous reason: one could hardly call that right. But if there is a hierarchy, then there can be one that is supreme. And when modern humankind is engulfed with shudders of nihilism at seeing the centre of the universe, empty and disenchanted (so that we almost want to flee back into excessive darkness), then this feeling is as insignificant as our indignation at the felled tree. Where did the feeling of homelessness come from? Where does this insight, which cannot be explained away, lurking in the most unlikely corners, come from? It is not true, this story, that reason explains everything. It is a mirage, the dream of the designed, managed and planned life. The religions of the world wash themselves before prayer, the mystics strive to cleanse their aura, the idealists dream of the creation of a new human being, the psychologists perceive man as a fragmented puzzle through sublimation, splitting off and repression. And you do not have to look far below the surface of society to feel that something is wrong. Something that many only feel when they have depression, suffer a burnout, or when their own death or that of a close relative looks them in the eye: that in their midst a crater gapes. That the vast mainland has been unmasked as a small island. And there's a storm going on outside.

LOST IN QADISHA

Of course I had to go for it. It was not in the stronghold of the Hezbollah militia; they were still a distance away. And the Syrian civil war had not yet started. I was quite clear and completely set on this journey. Only twenty, and all alone through Syria and then Lebanon, without a plan, with little money, sometimes trekking, sometimes hiking, always with a rucksack. These were not trips to the rebel-held areas in the south of the country or the Anti-Lebanon Mountains, nor were they solitary night wanderings through Beirut and Damascus. On the contrary: Lebanon had, for me, become sleepless nights spent bubbling the hookah, the smell of cardamom in coffee, the view over the colourful confusion of the souk of Tripoli and of the glittering sea, sitting alone on thousand-year-old ruins of Jbail, ancient Byblos, home of all books. Lebanon had shown me her enchanting side. Until this hike in the mountains.

Qadisha, 'the sacred', the sound of the name of a valley high in the northern mountain ranges of Lebanon. It had already been enough of an adventure, the way I got here, brought by some random people in a clapped-out old white Mercedes to just below the snow-capped peaks of the main Lebanon ridge. The next morning, the autumn sun breaks over the barren, white ridges. And below, encircled by these grey giants, the unheard-of silence of a green valley. A valley that tears down into the ragged ravine called *Qadisha*.

In inaudible space, a narrow waterfall falls on the rock face in a steep curve in the deep, unfathomable distance; the shady ridge of the winding gorge seems to be lost in the blue-grey, somewhere between the deeper regions and the horizon. The gorge lies in front of me, it goes down steeply, so steeply that the coniferous trees and shrubs seem to grow vertically out of the stones. Bees are buzzing around me, nobody seems awake. It promises to be a nice day. Only a pair of light trousers and a T-shirt, sandals and a small rucksack; I like travelling light. I had heard a great deal about this holy valley where saintly hermits had sought refuge from the noise of the world and built little monasteries, long before my journey. I do not have a map, but confidently I follow the next best path, which leads me turn by turn into the wet coolness between the protruding slopes. In one fell swoop it gets darker. Like entering a cathedral. I follow the central aisle deep into the nave and then on and on. For hours, and I meet nobody. All of the monasteries are abandoned, people do not seem to come over here often. Only a raven screams, yells and flutters out of the ruin.

I roam further into the wild romantic beauty of the Levantine mountain solitude. Beauty increasing in ferocity. The rocky outcrops seem increasingly jagged, and the little path that I follow leads higher and higher up above the valley floor, but also steeper and steeper up the stone slopes. It's long after noon. And to my astonishment, I have met no one. No one who might have given me information. Information, for example, about paths that lead back up the valley. I have not found one yet. Surprising, since I guess there are ways down in many places along the deep canyon.

Then comes the creeping transition from joy of adventure to growing concern. I count the hours it would take to get back if I turned back now. Twilight would begin in the late afternoon. And, finally, the transition from worry to dread. The sky is closing, the cloud cover closes over and it gets noticeably cooler. Suddenly there is nothing wildly romantic about this landscape anymore. It is only wild, it is scary. Soon it will no longer be cool up here, but bitterly cold. I will barely find my way in the dark. Barely survive a night in a T-shirt. The clouds are sinking lower, already they cover the upper edge of the valley in dark fog. The realization hits me with staggering weight: I have completely misjudged this. I had been fearless. Yet, in such a thoughtless way that could only be called foolish. It was folly that nearly cost me my life.

In the end, it is a miracle that saves me. I begin to cry out to God, thinking of Psalm 23: 'Even though I walk through the darkest valley, I will fear no evil'. But I'm afraid now. Not in the aforementioned biblical sense. I am scared, full of dread. I stand at a dead end, high up in the middle of the steep wall. The monastery to which the small path had led was as deserted as all the others, the doors tightly shut. The path ends here. Here, in front of the closed wooden gate, I scream out to God. Here, he saves me. For as I rush back along the path, headless and frantic with fear, I suddenly see a small coloured marker in the middle of the rock. I must have overlooked it before. It seems to point to a step in the stone. From this I clamber up a rocky crag. Behind it, something which looks like another step. Climbing with both hands and feet I ascend higher and higher. All around me fog. Far below me the dark valley. Just keep looking up and do not slip, as dizzying clefts open up beneath me. Outcrop by outcrop, foothold by foothold. Fingers cramp. My muscles are burning. And finally, am I really here? Breathless and sweaty, I actually reach a grassy spot. I can hardly believe my luck: I am actually here, up above again. Unimaginable if the *via ferrata* had gone elsewhere. Unimaginable, if I had fallen or hurt myself so badly that I could not have climbed on. Ashamed, pardoned, gifted, I stumbled back into my miserable quarters when deep night fell over *Bcharreh* and temperatures dropped almost to freezing.

It wasn't fearlessness on my part that led to this adventure. It was folly – folly that almost killed me. And it wasn't until I got scared that I realized this. It was simply unwise to underestimate this valley. It would have been wiser, safer and more enjoyable if I had inquired as to what kind of valley this was. How to equip myself for it. What to expect. Respect for such a wild wasteland, a certain knowledge of the danger: those were the only correct starting points for this hike. A little bit of fear would have spared me such dread. A reverence for *Qadisha*, the 'sacred', would have been the beginning of wisdom.

THE BEGINNING OF WISDOM

The Hebrew Bible speaks of a prerequisite for wisdom. It has something to do with recognizing value. If this condition is fulfilled, then man will be wise. And being wise means that his other value judgments, his life choices and his actions are also encompassed. But if this falls, then everything falls. If this falls, then man becomes foolish; he no longer recognizes the simplest things, his judgment is clouded and his life begins to fall apart in countless fractures. What the Bible calls 'wisdom' is not intellect, and 'folly' is not its absence. Even the cleverest people of this world can be foolish by God's standards. Wisdom and folly are questions of perspective and right weighting. If you can't see the wood for the trees, you will not be able to count the bark beetles on a trunk properly. 'Having lost sight of our goals, we redoubled our efforts,[18] says one proverb, with irony. Human life does not gain direction, a centre, a goal by the amassing of knowledge alone. That is what wisdom is all about.

The beginning of wisdom is the fear of the Lord, according to the Bible (Proverbs 9:10). The call to fear the Lord is found in many different places. 'You shall fear the LORD your God. You shall serve him and hold fast to him, and by his name you shall swear.' (Deuteronomy 10:20 ESV) And this is the beginning of a wise life? The fear of God? What exactly is this supposed to be? It is clear that first impressions are hardly positive. At first, this sounds like the Middle Ages, fear-filled religion, oppression and bondage. Fear and anxiety are generally considered bad guides. Who wants to be guided by fear? People who are driven by fear are at best called unstable, in the worst cases mentally ill. And then, afraid of what – God?! Is not the idea of a punitive heavenly ruler, an all-righteous despot petty-mindedly observing any commandment, the most expendable of all mythical figures? A primeval spectre with cringing, creeping, unenlightened subjects? It is this kind of image of God from which those who turn their backs on faith flee. And it is one – combined with a correspondingly austere works-and-punishment teaching of the church – that has caused a whole generation of theologians and clerics to stand up for something else.

Is that what the Bible means?

Looking at the Old Testament, it stands out immediately that humankind is drawn differently, consistently so. The small-minded, oppressed man who is deprived of his life: nothing could be further from the world of the Old Testament. God crowns man, calls him to greatness and dignity, rejoices in him, bestows him. So why 'fear'? Why not a level partnership? According to biblical understanding, the coexistence of God and man only works if the realities remain clear. The writer of Ecclesiastes says, laconically:

18 Attributed to the novelist Mark Twain.

God is in heaven
  and you are on earth,
  so let your words be few.
ECCLESIASTES 5:2B

Here it becomes gradually clear what the Bible means by 'fear of the Lord'. The Hebrew word means more than 'fear'. It means awesome knowledge of what to do with fear. It means the fear that does not spring from a frightful being, but from clear knowledge.

If you stand on a high tower, you would be well advised to hold on. Anyone preparing to buy a house has every reason to respect the large sum of money involved. This kind of fear means I have an idea that I am dealing with something much more powerful than me. This is not self-deprecation, but a completely clear appraisal of one's own situation.

This is exactly the feeling that religious philosopher Rudolf Otto describes as being the most basic category of religious experience. A sense of the numinous.

The creature feeling: the emotion of a creature, abased and overwhelmed by its own nothingness in contrast to that which is supreme above all creatures.[19]

Realizing that one is a creature, limited, on an island surrounded by the ocean. It is that feeling which can be sensed in the scary, the feeling of the uncanny. That which frightens and irresistibly attracts every child at the same time. The comprehensive intuition that the world has its secrets. And that we are not at home here. That there is more beyond the visible. It did not escape Goethe's attention that this is more than a marginal phenomenon of life:

The shudder's the truest sign of humanity: Though the world is such we may not feel it, Once seized by it, we feel Immensity deeply.[20]

19 Rudolf Otto, *The Idea of the Holy* (Oxford University Press, 1929), p.1.
20 Johann Wolfgang von Goethe, *Faust, Part II*, Act I Scene V, 6272–6274.

This feeling is the basis of all religion. And it does not deceive. In fact, man is not the author and centre of the universe. He is a creature. Limited by lifetime, knowledge and power on every corner. He does well not to think too highly of himself. Who he is, and who he is not, should not be forgotten. It is appropriate to think of the distance between God and him as infinite, insurmountable. No, God is not a friendly neighbour to be patted on the back. Such an idea is not only incomplete; it is profoundly blind. Anyone who underestimates the depth of the canyon at the edge of which he is standing is not brave when he jumps. He is foolish. Only those who know nothing about canyons and gravity do not realize this. And to know what it means as a human to face a God who is omnipotent, uncreated, eternal and holy, is rightly inspiring of fear. This is not the spawn of a frightened soul, but clearly outlined reality.

It is the beginning of wisdom; it is the fear of God.

What of the fear of God in our time? Has not our sense of the majesty of God been lost to our world and to our churches? That it has been lost to the world is tragic. It is easy to complain: 'The young people are no longer spiritual,' some might say (perhaps one who is not so pious himself). But is it only, or even primarily, a problem of secular society? Looking at the Bible, it is striking that, amazingly often, 'God's own staff' are responsible for the whole nation going astray. In the book of the prophet Hosea, God says, 'My people are destroyed for lack of knowledge' (Hosea 4:6a NKJV). He means the knowledge of God.

> *Because you have rejected knowledge,*
> *I will also reject you from being a priest for Me;*
> *Because you have forgotten the law of your God ...*
> HOSEA 4:6B NKJV

Again and again, the prophets reproached the priests and the scribes as being responsible. If the theologians and believers no longer fear God, it seems to have an automatic impact on a whole society. And so renewal must always begin in the house of God: in the church, we would say today.

But what is the consequence when someone adopts this 'beginning of wisdom'? What kind of person will they become? Clearly a God-fearing one. But whoever imagines a bloodless cleric will once again be taught a lesson by the book of Proverbs: the knowledge of God, the fear of the Lord is, according to biblical thought, neither restrictive nor compulsive, but instead is called a fountain of life and a rescue from deadly snares (Proverbs 14:27). It brings life, it gives freedom and tears the chains from the heart that they bind. Believers are called to the fear of the Lord in the Psalms, 'for those who fear him lack nothing' (Psalm 34:9). Lack nothing? This can hardly mean material abundance; but apparently, a life in a state of deep sufficiency, of an inner wealth, which is dependent on the fear of the Lord. It is described as leading to life (Proverbs 19:23), 'its wages are riches and honour and life' (Proverbs 22:4). An extravagant promise for something that appeared so unwelcoming at first glance! But could it be that the Bible is right? That the rediscovery of reverence and respect for the majesty of God is the key to a full and joyful life?

FAREWELL CHEAP 'GOD'!

While the good-natured pastor preaches a sermon on how the rainbow is a sign of hope for all people, calling for more compassion and assuring the faithful that Jesus' drastic words in the gospels on hell and judgment are just pictures and his miracles by no means historical facts, a young man in the vicinity surfs the internet to learn about voodoo. The service is taking place late morning in a well-heated church. Fasting, giving and premarital abstinence are never preached about here, and every worshipper can be reassured: here these things are never talked about. At the beginning of the school year, all the children are brought to the front to receive a gift from the deacon, and later in the afternoon is the blessing of the pets. In a neighbouring monastery, a course for meditative painting takes place, and in every station bookstore we can inform ourselves that a hike to Santiago de Compostela enhances one's holistic development. Fast only if it helps to detox. Repent only if we feel psychologically compensated; in other words if it makes us feel better. The 'let's talk about it' spirituality instead of praying. Prayer not as an act of worship, but as a friendly chat. Spiritual practice that does not fit with the profile of today's wellness religion, that only disturbs our spiritual comfort zone.

We have made spirituality cheap because we have made God cheap. We sell a god without laws, without requirements, without judgment, without hell. A god who can be hoodwinked. Who agrees and sings along happily when it goes: 'We are all going to heaven, because we are nice people'. A god in which all religions are paths to the truth, and a god who is people-friendly. And by that we mean that he cannot be a danger to us because he does not have any other intention but that of supporting our ego. Who, at most, has his own opinion on issues relating to environmental protection and globalization, but otherwise only appears in our lives when it comes to supporting and to blessing us. A god who makes no demands. Happy messages instead of threatening messages! No longer afraid of the loving god, the harmless monarch, who somehow does not intervene in the legislation of his country. But what you cannot fear, you cannot worship. Which was already clear, and no one should be surprised. Over a toothless god, who would not harm one single fly, one can perhaps smile. But he will not seize hold of anyone too deeply. A benevolent old man, somewhere in heaven, or perhaps just a semi-astral existence of metaphysical matter in the world of ideas, a god who will not inspire anyone to any great sacrifice. Today the faith of the builders of gothic cathedrals is unimaginable. The artist himself is often anonymous, even to this day. The financiers sometimes did not live to see the completion of the building, but their main concern was that the building was finished. What a contrast to our selfie culture! The ego just wasn't the centre of attention! The greatness and dignity of the contributor is precisely that he forgets himself for the sake of a higher purpose.

The one who considers himself at the centre of everything has lost much more than the truth. They lose beauty, pleasure and the enjoyment of sharing in something in which they forget themselves. Yes, as Hans Urs von Balthasar and C.S. Lewis aptly state, the fixation with their own sensibility destroys the feeling of pleasure in something beautiful. Anyone who experiences an opera or kisses their loved one simply spoils the whole event by analyzing themselves. The idea is bizarre. *He buries his hands in her blonde locks, his lips are approaching, millimetre by millimetre, in his head the thought: 'Interesting, I suddenly have an expectation of a joyful feeling, one that I have previously experienced, and which also occurred when I was in a similar situation.'* Or, the peculiar contemporary who pays no heed to the swelling of the strings for the overture, the warm entry of the woodwind to the melody of the *leitmotif*, the gravity-defying quiver of the stage curtain as it is raised for the first act, but is only aware that his left eye sees things a little worse than the right one. They need to reassess enjoyment as self-fixation robs them of what they want to experience. But they can achieve everything when they are 'all ears'. That is if they do not think about themselves at all. If they can forget themselves and get fully absorbed in the opera, or their lover.

We read in the Psalms:

> *Great is the LORD and most worthy of praise;*
> *his greatness no one can fathom.*
> PSALM 145:3

And if we believe the Bible, then God is the most wholly fascinating, the most exalted of all. The most worthy of fear, amazement and pleasure. But all that is lost when we downplay God. When we put ourselves in the centre. When in the church, the gospel and our faith is always and only about man. If we only carry an image of God that does not get in the way of this self. Adapt it to what suits us. To make it compatible with our ego. Trivialize him. Or talk about anything and everything else. Yes, it may have been necessary to counter that fearful image of God with compassion and philanthropy, as balance. But this is done more times than not! How often does it become a complete pendulum swing to the opposite extreme? How often the complete trivialization of God? But a god one can't be afraid of is terribly boring. He does not kindle astonishment, admiration or delight. What you cannot fear, you will not bow the knee before.

And so if we lose the fear of God, worship also gives way. We have painted for ourselves a picture of a tamed god. But a tamed god is no god at all. He is an illusion, the work of man, an idol. And from each of these images, nothing presents itself more than an idealized version of ourselves. No wonder that such a god fascinates no one. No wonder nothing grows on such ground. What costs nothing is worth nothing. Compromise and convenience have never grown anything worth living and fighting for. It's time to break out of the religious comfort zone.

3

PRIORITY

THE FOLLY OF THE HEART

All worldly questions are trivial compared to the question of whether God exists and what he is like. If he exists, all other questions find their value in this first question. For those who have boarded a train, it's hardly a trivial question to ask where that train is actually going. Someone who replies with 'What an irrelevant question!' would be called an idiot. Maybe they are so busy enjoying the ride that it never occurs to them to think about an alleged direction or destination, or to consider whether these even exist at all. If a cruise liner is heading at full speed straight for something that might be an iceberg, then many questions are suddenly of secondary importance. The question of whether it really is an iceberg is the only important one. The captain might well be accused of having been struck with blindness, or of being completely deluded, if he were to take the decision to first see that the deck is swabbed or that an engine test is carried out. An old word for such a state of blindness or delusion is 'folly'. And it is precisely this concept that the Bible applies to those who deny God. This may not sound very friendly, but what is meant here is not a personal devaluation of people who are not religious. What is meant is that people who do not think about God are not just missing information, rather their hearts are fundamentally warped. The fact that a created being forgets that its very existence has not arisen out of itself, the psalmist can only acknowledge with incredulity. Shaking his head in despair he writes: 'The fool says in his heart, "There is no God".' (Psalm 14:1) It is folly, it is loss of reality, it is the repression of something obvious. But it's something the fool says in their heart, not in their mind. It seems to be about a deeper, more urgent decision, which precedes the unbelief of the mind. It is out of a not-wanting-to-believe, a not-wanting-to-see, that the heart may have decided, for reasons perhaps not fully known by the mind. A detailed discussion of atheism will not be attempted here. However, there are very few people who would say categorically and with certainty that there is no God. The majority of people are simply living in such a way that they just never think about exactly what they believe. About who exactly God is. Or how we might come by some meaningful explanation and whether there are any reliable answers.

A GUEST IN A CURIOUS RESTAURANT

The question of God is central. And once again, there is a clear expectation that the answer will be part of the standard repertoire of those who gather in his name and believe in him. But how about this for a simple comparison: imagine a hungry person entering a restaurant. Although they do not yet know exactly what they want to eat, or even what there is available here, their hunger drives them on. The facade of the restaurant is inviting. A luxuriant vine graces the entrance, pictures in the foyer show artfully designed desserts, magnificent roasts and various fine appetizers. Anticipation is rising. The customer is welcomed by a friendly waiter, who quickly shows him to a comfortable place by the window. The tasteful arrangement of tablecloth, folded cloth napkins, fresh flowers and a newly-lit candle is delightful. The soft lighting bathes the dark red velvet walls in warmth and the sound of a classical piano in the background adds a celebratory touch to an otherwise homely atmosphere. When he has made himself comfortable, the customer naturally wishes to take a look at the menu. After the initial welcome, however, none of the numerous waiters approach. In fact, nobody seems to notice him here. Following persistent hand signals, eventually a friendly middle-aged waitress appears: how can she help? Her hair is perfect, her clothes elegant yet not stiff, her demeanour perfectly accomplished.

'I just wondered whether you could please bring a menu?'

A slightly irritated look, then a hesitant answer: 'Ah, a menu, yes, such a thing would have to be somewhere. Why do you need it? It is not exactly the most common request.'

Now feeling a bit unsure, the customer replies that he could, of course, just order, but he would first like to know what there is to eat and drink. These words seem to have an immediate impact on the waitress. 'Oh you want to eat? That really is not what we are set up for, basically that would be possible but ...'

'But this is a restaurant, isn't it?' the customer replies.

Of course, the customer is completely right, the desire for food is understandable and by no means absurd. It's just that neither the waitress nor her current colleagues are well versed in the hospitality industry. She will have to make further enquiries.

Now rather bemused, the customer asks what sort of restaurant this is, when questions about food seem to be so unusual. No, no – one would not want to create the wrong impression, so the waitress really tries very hard. The establishment simply focuses more on the visual design of the restaurant and on the friendliness of the service staff, although in the past someone who knew about the food industry did actually work there. It is still said that during the founding years of the restaurant, it was very common that guests were actually served food. But they only know this from hearsay, according to the waitress.

Anyway, she lacks expertise in the food industry, and so she will ask her colleagues without hesitation as to whether anyone knows anything about menus or food in general. Then it will become feasible and within the realms of possibility that they might produce food from somewhere.

A restaurant is there for people to eat in. A restaurant does not make sense when hungry people are unable to get food there. And above all other qualifications, a waiter, waitress or bartender needs to know what food and beverages are available. All other questions and all services offered only gain their meaning when this is clear.

Everything in the church is about God. A church does not make sense if God does not exist. But neither does a church make sense if no one who gathers there can give any knowledge of God. If there are nice curtains, friendly staff and a heater in the restaurant, then that is good in itself, but all this could be anywhere. If there is nothing to eat there, you may as well just go to a bookshop, the waiting room of an orthodontist or the cinema. A restaurant is characterized by the fact that food is served there. And if people in the church do not find anyone who knows God, they will not stay there, even with beautiful architecture or friendly staff. In the long term, they will hardly remain just for beautiful music, edifying words or warm fellowship. Because all of this can be found elsewhere and it is often far better. Of course, it is not the case that God is not present in his church, as if he were some form of exotic incense or a highly rare, fine antique lamp. God is not hard to find, he wants to be sought after and he can be found. However, it is *people* who either direct others to him, or block them from finding the way to him. The waitress is not the food herself, but she is the mediator between the hungry customer and the master chef. And it's alarming when the waitress does not know anything about the food. But even more alarming is when Christians know nothing about God, or have only a theoretical knowledge. What good is it if the waitress can explain all the differences between a medium fillet steak and a fried rib-eye steak, and yet cannot take an order?

A LACK OF WORDS

Our forgetfulness of God manifests itself in our churches in two ways: by saying nothing at all, and by theorizing. Let's begin with the first, a widespread symptom. A churchgoer (or even a priest, pastor or theologian) is spontaneously interviewed in the street about their thoughts on the holiness of God. What are their opinions on this? The question would be startling to many. The holiness of God ... is there much to say about it? For that you would have to be a theologian. But would someone like this have more to say? Or about how the omnipotence of God might be reconciled with his grace and love? Should one even comment on something like this spontaneously? Even better informed Christians would probably falter after a few sentences.

Change of scene. One of the persons interviewed is an enthusiastic amateur gardener, another is a dedicated racing cyclist and a third has a software development company. If you were to ask the gardener for the secret of their particularly beautiful flowering roses, you would probably find yourself in a long conversation. What is there to know! It depends on the variety of rose and the location. On the best fertilizer and on the correct way to prune. There is so much to observe! It would not be very different if you asked the athlete for the brand of his racing bike and his favourite rides. From brake mechanics to gears, from fitness drinks to helmets, favourite Alpine passes to best times: there is so much to tell. Jesus said, 'For the mouth speaks what the heart is full of.' (Luke 6:45) And the newly-in-love can talk endlessly about 'the one' and does not understand at all why others do not find them equally interesting. Just as programmers simply cannot understand why anyone can find a lengthy four-hundred-page manual about programming language completely uninteresting. Anyone who is captivated by a subject has something to say about it. And someone who has nothing to say about it, has probably not been impacted by it. Their heart is not full of it.

The silence of Christians about God is more eloquent than what they say about him. For what do you say about him? Little that is wrong. But very little at all. Our problem is not heresy, the false doctrine of God; it is the total absence of talk of him, either true or false. But a waiter who does not speak of food because he himself has no idea, will not arouse anyone's appetite. He will not appeal to the hungry and will not whet the appetite of those who are not yet hungry.

The lack of words is a lack of love. A marriage in which none of the partners has ever been unfaithful, but where there are no words of love, is not convincing as an example of a loving union. Whoever wishes to do good to another, but never says good things to them, does not encourage them, does not reward them, does not thank them, does not mention their merits and cannot express their joy over them; it follows that their ability to love is underdeveloped. Because one who loves – one who really loves – finds words. The newly-in-love want to hear everything from each other, tell each other everything, talk on the phone for hours on end and write endless letters. And if someone is less eloquent and occasionally words fail them and they are unable to describe the depth of feeling that has grown within them, they stammer away, even if only with the painful assertion that their real meaning cannot be articulated. The desire to say so much more is a torment to the one who loves. To the one who *knows*. Who *knows* the one he loves. And our silence about God, our talk about anything but him, betrays that we do not know him and do not love him. At least much less than all the people and things that overflow from our hearts.

TECHNICAL REASON

Of course, there are those who are knowledgeable. We like to refer to them in the same way as the waitress does the 'experts' among her colleagues. They know their subject. And indeed, there are more than a handful of books written about God, and people do concern themselves with religion, philosophy and that which is beyond them. As to knowing, of course, that is different. For example, I know that Madagascar is a pretty poor country. I know because I have read or been told about it. My knowledge is correct, and yet, it is by no means like the knowledge of a missionary who has lived there for a long time. They have experienced the situation personally, it is an immediate, direct familiarity with the location.

We live in a so-called Information Society. By this is meant that the digitally available knowledge about almost everything has doubled over the course of a few years or even months and is often quickly overtaken by more up-to-date information. And that most of this knowledge is available to everyone. At the press of a button, I know the population of Madagascar, the rainfall, the name of the highest mountains and the average life expectancy of the inhabitants. And yet, from this knowledge springs the kind of reason which in the first chapter was called 'technical' or 'scientific' reason. It is reason that makes knowledge available faster than it can actually be appropriated. Reason, the actual confrontation with the object, is no longer a prerequisite to possess proper 'knowledge' of the object. It is arbitrary, reproducible knowledge in which that which is known can remain completely distant. I do not have to relate to it, neither do I have to listen to a person's story, travel to another place, peer through a telescope, smell the blossom or feel the sensation of desert sand between my toes. The digital reason of the digital age, numbers on screens.

Ignatius of Loyola knew that, 'What fills and satisfies the soul consists not in knowing much, but in our understanding the realities profoundly and in savouring them interiorly'.[21] And we know it too. Everyone knows the difference between a traveller's eyewitness report and statistics on Wikipedia. The latter provides us with knowledge, but the former grabs us and does much more than just inform. It draws you in. The traveller's personal experience becomes, as it were, a door that also opens up something to me that I could not enter in to on my own through mere data. It is precisely this metaphor that Jesus uses in his harsh criticism of the theologians and clergymen of his time:

> 'Woe to you experts in the law, because you have taken away the key to knowledge. You yourselves have not entered, and you have hindered those who were entering.'
> LUKE 11:52

Interesting doubling of the accusation. At first, it relates only to you personally: even though there was something open to you, you did not want to enter. But now, by not entering, you have prevented others from entering. If you have not experienced something yourself, then you will not be able to convey the experience to others. He who does not himself burn, will not ignite others. Or turned positively and to quote Augustine: 'Only those who burn themselves can kindle fire in others.'

Wherever Scripture speaks of knowledge, it means knowledge of God. But there is also knowledge about oneself, the need for repentance, the requirements of a completely changed life. Both the Hebrew and Greek scriptures of the Bible use a charmingly ambiguous word for 'knowledge'. It is a word that occurs at the very beginning, in the creation story: 'Now Adam knew Eve his wife, and she conceived and bore Cain' (Genesis 4:1a NKJV). It is obvious what is meant here. So intellectual knowledge and union of the sexes both have the same word? Yes, that's the

---

21 Second annotation of *Spiritual exercises of St Ignatius of Loyola*: A translation and commentary by George E Ganss, SJ (Loyola Press, 1992), p.22.

Bible! And it shows how much more is meant by 'knowledge'. Far from being just intellectual information, biblical knowledge means something holistic. The union with something else, a union that gives life to something new. In glaring contrast to the digitally reproduced knowledge of the 'copy-and-paste'. Here something happens that is deeply personal, that touches the heart of the human being, and from which something categorically new arises. This is biblical understanding. And that's exactly what God meant when, in the book of Hosea, he suddenly comes out with: 'I want your constant love, not your animal sacrifices. I would rather have my people know me than burn offerings to me.' (Hosea 6:6 GNT) He is not interested in external ritual. And he's not interested in dry theology. He actually wants to be known.

Let us know,
Let us pursue the knowledge of the LORD.
HOSEA 6:3A NKJV

Such is the reaction of those who have realized what God really is interested in. In a knowing of God that makes it impossible for us to be pushed into an impersonal relationship with him. Because at least Jesus could hardly accuse the scribes of a lack of words. There was an inflation of theological theorizing and ritualistic reasoning. But knowledge that does not affect me existentially, into which I myself do not enter, is not God's knowledge, but rather a deceptive replacement. A substitute that wholeheartedly fools the starving, and likewise my own heart. There is no sustenance there! And precisely because it has not become an intimate and living knowledge for me, means I am even more of a hindrance to people than a help. This fiasco would have been easier to see through, if it were not for a waiter who talks a lot about food when in fact he has no access to any food.

4

GLORY

A SELF-FORGETFUL GOD?

If the question of what God is like is the most crucial question confronting all humanity and the entire Christian church, this in itself does not prove that God himself attaches great importance to it. Being overly focused on the centrality of God could in itself become a dangerous error. Gazing mystically up into the heavens when Jesus taught the way of practical neighbourly love? Some might speculate, perhaps, that it is not so important to God himself that we should consider him, as long as we are good people. After all, what use is a person who lives with his head so much in the clouds that, here on earth, people's mundane lives only get in his way? And finally, aren't there already enough weird saints and fanatics who, in the name of the divine, make life in this world hell for others? Doesn't true knowledge of God mean turning to your neighbour and having the courage to descend from the heady heights of theology to the real plight of your fellow human beings?

Wouldn't that be fulfilment of the phrase 'God is love'; to be unmindful of himself and unconcerned with his own reputation? In the end, isn't every good Christian simply a humanist performing practical acts of charity?

So what is important to God himself? What motivates him, if one can ask that? Many possible statements come to mind. God is Creator, he is Saviour and Deliverer. God is loving Father. The highest moral authority. All these statements are true, but they only describe the essence of God in relation to people. God has created, redeemed and freed people. He is their loving Father and shows them the way of life. God is all of these for humankind. What joy and happiness that it is so! And still the Grand Canyon doesn't first become majestic in order to be a backdrop to the selfie. It already is so, in and of itself. And even if it were not, the two giggling 15-year-old girls would not make it so with their smartphones. God is the God of eternity. The decision to create the world springs freely from his heart. Nobody forced him to do it, there is no higher law that would have obliged him to do so. He is the highest law, nothing is above him. His motivation and what is important to him, therefore, cannot be something that only comes into being by his creative act. It has to be found within his own being.

MEZUZAH

On entering a house, when putting on his robes at the beginning of prayers and even when going to sleep, the devout Jew will recite the central confession of the Jewish faith, imprinted on his mind by tens of thousands of repetitions, the *Sh'ma*. '*Sh'ma Yisrael Adonai Eloheinu Adonai Echad*': 'Hear, O Israel: the LORD our God, the LORD is one.' (Deuteronomy 6:4) It stands at the beginning of the recital of God's commandments and is in the small capsule on the doorway of a Jewish house, the *mezuzah*. When he was asked about the most important commandment – the most important of all – Jesus replies with these very words (Mark 12:29). But what does the statement 'the God of Israel is *one*' mean? Does it mean an intolerant rejection of other religions? A call to accept nothing more than the imposing brute force of a despotic god? Conversion by force is as foreign to Judaism as it is in the New Testament. It can never be about forcing people into a realization. How would that work? The confession of lips alone is not what God desires;[22] certainly not a forced confession. So that cannot be the meaning of *echad*. The word is often translated as 'the only God'. Is this term simply a rejection of polytheism? In fact, Old Testament scholars disagree about exactly when strict monotheism was established in Israel. Forces and powers, Elohim and Baalim, idols and the sons of the gods: the Semitic psyche is full of these. The question of whether there is only one heavenly being does not seem to be foremost. But central is the statement: YHWH is *echad* among all of you. Not only that he should be the only one you worship, but that he IS actually *echad*. *Echad* means one and only. Not comparable with others, he stands in a different category, plays in a different league. And one in which there is no opponent; he occupies a category that nobody else inhabits. *Echad* does not only mean that there is no other god, but that he is all that he is, in and of himself. There is no one who caused him to be. He is not dependent on any cause. There is nothing that influences him. He requires no reason and no external rationale. He is one with himself, and in himself alone. It also means that there is no complicated conglomeration of opposing tendencies and diverging currents. God is that simplest and least complex of beings. Everything created shows traces of growth or emergence. Traces of decline or decay. Has parts and sides. He has his being of himself and not by anyone agreeing or choosing him to be God. If all human beings on earth decided to become atheists, that would not change God's existence any more than the existence of the sun would be threatened by the fact that all men chose to gouge out their eyes.[23] He is also not dependent on a particular people who worship him, or who *should* worship him. God is worthy of worship because he is *echad*. The command that follows

22 Isaiah 29:13; Matthew 15:8.
23 Aiden Wilson Tozer, *The Attributes of God: The Knowledge of the Holy* (CreateSpace Independent Publishing Platform, 2018).

directly on in the text, to 'Love the LORD your God with all your heart and with all your soul and with all your strength' (Deuteronomy 6:5), is nothing more than a completely plausible conclusion. God is one and only.

GOD'S HAPPINESS

That God is *echad* is not only the central proposition of the Judaeo-Christian creed. Because what this creed affirms, if it proclaims truth, can only be something with a completely independent existence from itself. And this is the fact that God is happy.[24] That God is happy? Yes, you read that correctly. In the first volume of his book *Summa Contra Gentiles,* the greatest theologian of the Middle Ages, Thomas Aquinas, sets out what one can say about God and how one can speak about him. Starting with atheistic, Islamic and Jewish criticism of Christian teaching, he develops a basis for religious belief based equally on argument and Scripture which is still unparalleled. The first volume of the book is essentially about God. The possible proofs of his existence, his omnipotence and his eternity. But even on the last pages of this monumental first part, it seems to become more intense. After complex discussion about being and non-being in God, there is a clearly accentuated conclusion. Chapter 100 is titled '*Quod deus est beatus*'. In English, '*God is happy*'. And he follows this in Chapter 101 with the title '*God is his happiness*'. And in his otherwise sober style and his sometimes dry philosophical analysis, Aquinas, in the last chapter, seems to turn to a play on words. The last heading shouts it out: '*The happiness of God is perfect and unique and transcends every other happiness*'. And a few lines later: '*God is so happy beyond all else in an incomparable way*'.[25] God is so happy?

24 Translator's note: In many translations of Aquinas, and the pieces referred to in this section, the word used is translated 'blessed' in English – Chapter 100, 'That God is blessed; Chapter 101, 'That God in his blessedness' and in 102, 'That the perfect and unique blessedness of God excels every other blessedness'; 'God is in a unique way perfectly blessed.' However, the concept Aquinas is referring to, and the word which is translated 'blessed' in most versions of the Bible, means 'happy' in both Greek and Hebrew and is translated 'happy' in the Good News Translation. See for example, Matthew 5.
25 Thomas Aquinas, *Summa contra gentiles*, 102, translated by Anton C Pegis (Hanover House, 1955).

What do joy and happiness mean? We are happy in the moment, when things are going well. When there's nothing more to be desired. Joy is the feeling that comes when *something* or *someone* is present. The object of that happiness and joy is not the joy or happiness itself. They are simply an emotional reaction to the fact that that something is there. Something that we would love to continue to be there. The sight of my child gives me joy. I feel joy when a friend who has returned from a long journey comes to visit. I enjoy a good red wine, and the attic conversion, finished at long last, gives me joy. Joy tells us that it is good that it is so. It is good that the child is there, that my friend is there, that the wine is there and, where previously there was only an empty loft space, a bedroom and a bathroom are there. Joy sees something and recognizes it as good. In that sense, we can assume that God had joy as the first feeling in connection with his creation: 'God saw all that he had made, and it was very good' (Genesis 1:31a). Joy is joy in what it is; joy needs no further cause. 'Why are you happy that your child is well again?' Is a question no mother would understand: 'Well, because he's my child.' 'And why are you planting roses in your garden?' 'Because I like them and they give me pleasure.' 'And what does it bring you, this joy? What is the point of joy?' Nobody asks that, for joy rejoices in what it is. And joy needs no purpose; that in which it rejoices, is purpose enough. There is no why.

God is a God of joy. His decision to create the world springs from his own heart. A spontaneous, voluntary act without ulterior motive. God gives life. And he sees it, and is happy about it. Reason enough for him to have created something! And, in fact, we read exactly this about God in the Bible. Paul proclaims 'the gospel concerning the glory of the blessed God' (1 Timothy 1:11b). The word used here in Greek is *makarios* and means happy, God is happy. The Psalms paint a similar picture:

> *Our God is in heaven;*
> *he does whatever pleases him.*
> PSALM 115:3

*The L*ORD* foils the plans of the nations;*
    he thwarts the purposes of the peoples.
*But the plans of the L*ORD* stand firm for ever,*
    the purposes of his heart through all generations.
PSALM 33:10–11

It is an image of God at peace with himself, without care, that is described here. A God relatively unmoved by the raging of people and the refusal of people to recognize him as sovereign. His response to the kings of the earth uniting against him:

The One enthroned in heaven laughs.
PSALM 2:4

You will fill me with joy in your presence,
with eternal pleasures at your right hand.
PSALM 16:11B

But what is God happy about? Joy, as defined earlier, is simply the feeling, of seeing, tasting or experiencing something and finding that it is good. One might also say, when we recognize the being or essence of something and affirm it. Whom can God recognize and affirm before Creation? In what does he rejoice? What does he affirm?

The truest and the most educated of people will recognize greatness and dignity where greatness and dignity are present. They do not allow themselves to be blinded and seduced by false authorities. But they do recognize those who are genuinely awe-inspiring, when they really do exist. God is not only *echad*, the exalted, the sublime sovereign and, above all, worthy; but also the most truthful and the one who knows most about being awe-inspiring. God rejoices in himself, and because he is only truth, the value that is objectively the highest value of the universe is the most important to him: his own.

•˙•˛•˙•˙•˛•˙•● ●˙•˙•˛•˙•˙•˙

A DIVINE EGOMANIAC?

Some readers may have noticed a conundrum in the last few sentences. A God who is concerned about his own honour? Is it not a characteristic of love that you do not seek your own honour? This, however, is the enduring testimony of Scripture: God upholds his own honour, for the sake of his own name, to reveal his glory. Exactly this concept is found in countless places in the Bible:

God creates people and nations in his glory:

> 'everyone who is called by my name,
>   whom I created for my glory,
>   whom I formed and made.'
>
> ISAIAH 43:7

He chooses Israel to show his glory to the nations:

> He said to me, 'You are my servant,
>   Israel, in whom I will display my splendour.'
>
> ISAIAH 49:3

He makes known his holy name through his saving of his people:

> But for the sake of my name, I brought them out of Egypt.
> I did it to keep my name from being profaned in the eyes
> of the nations among whom they lived and in whose sight
> I had revealed myself to the Israelites.
>
> EZEKIEL 20:9

He gives us commandments that his name be sanctified:

> Do not profane my holy name, for I must be acknowledged
> as holy by the Israelites. I am the LORD, who made you
> holy.
>
> LEVITICUS 22:32

For his great name's sake, he acts graciously towards Israel:

> For the sake of his great name the LORD will not reject his
> people, because the LORD was pleased to make you his own.
>
> 1 SAMUEL 12:22

He forgives the sinner who flees to him:

> *For the sake of your name, L*ORD*,*
> *forgive my iniquity, though it is great.*
> PSALM 25:11

The reason for the construction of the temple is so that his glory is seen (1 Kings 8:41–45). The reason why God preserves Jerusalem is the honour of his own name (2 Kings 19:34; 20:6). It is precisely this honour that motivates him to gather his people out of their exile (Ezekiel 36:22–32). Jesus describes exactly the same reason for his coming:

> *'Now my soul is troubled, and what shall I say? "Father, save me from this hour"? No, it was for this very reason I came to this hour. Father, glorify your name!' Then a voice came from heaven, 'I have glorified it, and will glorify it again.'*
> JOHN 12:27–28

So God is concerned about his own honour. But why? Does he have low self-esteem? Does he have opponents? Is he dependent on praise and acknowledgement from grovelling servants? But if so, why does he then create people who can also decide against him? Why not just robots who cannot help but sing constant *Hosannas* to him?

HONOUR, TRIUNE

Crucial to the understanding of God's preoccupation with his own honour are two fundamental statements of the Christian understanding of God. Firstly, the statement that God is triune, and secondly, the statement that God reveals himself. The doctrine of the Trinity of God does not say that there are three gods. Rather, it grew out of the experience of the early church that Jesus of Nazareth, on the one hand, called God his Father and prayed to him, but on the other hand also spoke of being one with the Father, acting on his behalf. He forgave sins, reinterpreted the law ('But I tell you that ...' Matthew 5:22), raised the dead: only God can do all that. In Jesus Christ, God became man. The Father sends the Holy Spirit: in this way the love of God is poured into our hearts. Not just power, but spiritual power. How are we to think of this? Christian theology has traversed many paths to bring us closer to this profound mystery. But everything revolves around the simple statement that God is love (1 John 4:8). But who does God love when there is no one to love? And before creation, in whom was this God able to rejoice? Is he a lonely God? The One and only, yes. In the breathtaking wasteland of his heavenly palaces where no one lives? A God who is love but, sadly, has no one to love? What exactly is joy actually rejoicing in, in a physical other? What kind of a love would this be, that has no one as a lover?

The doctrine of the Trinity says that there is already fellowship in God. Because love is not just a feeling. Love is also an act, a deed. Love gives itself away. And perfect love gives itself away completely. God is perfect love and gives himself away completely. The Father gives himself entirely away eternally, in the Son. Eternal love between Father and Son long before the beginning of the universe. The Father loves the Son and rejoices in him. The Son honours the Father and rejoices in him. The joy, the love and the knowing of each is so dynamic, so genuine, so personal and so real that it is itself a divine person: the Holy Spirit. None of the three divine persons exist 'only for themselves'. There are not three gods. They are simply the essence of love. This love gives itself, receives, and creates a third, 'togetherness'. It is simply the essence of joy. It wants to give itself, allows itself to be given and holds a feast. Yes, God is concerned for his own honour, but the way he deals with this is to give himself away. God does not regard his rights in an egotistical way. Instead, long before there were people who could ever honour him, there was in God the love of the Father for the Son. And that is the testimony of Jesus: for him it did not need to be about his own honour, because that's what the Father is all about: 'I am not seeking glory for myself; but there is one who seeks it, and he is the judge.' (John 8:50)

Notice Jesus does not need recognition from people, because he is secure in the assurance of his Father's recognition. But he is also not saying that he does not seek any honour or recognition at all. He knows that honour is rightly due to him. He knows that the Father honours him (John 8:54). But he does not demand honour from men, whether through manipulation, exhibitionism or violence.

And finally, the Holy Spirit:

> 'But when he, the Spirit of truth, comes, he will guide you into all the truth. He will not speak on his own; he will speak only what he hears, and he will tell you what is yet to come. He will glorify me because it is from me that he will receive what he will make known to you. All that belongs to the Father is mine. That is why I said the Spirit will receive from me what he will make known to you.'
>
> JOHN 16:13–15

The Father and the Holy Spirit honour Jesus, the Son. And the Son honours the Father, even unto death:

> After Jesus said this, he looked towards heaven and prayed: 'Father, the hour has come. Glorify your Son, that your Son may glorify you.'
>
> JOHN 17:1

WHAT THE WHOLE STORY TELLS OF

God's esteem for his own glory is not the egocentricity of a narcissistically disturbed pasha, firstly because God in himself is already threefold, each one honouring the others and putting the others first, and secondly because he unveils his glory. He shows all his cards. He makes himself known. He displays his nature. He doesn't only demand obedience, he also shows why he deserves it. A majestic and sovereign God could easily enforce worship. He could create creatures for whom there is no other choice. But he could also create people like us and shake them with such overwhelming force that they could not help but to beat their breasts and fall prostate. God, however, chooses another way. If, as has been argued, God is by his very nature an exalted and happy God, then the reason for creating must be sought within himself. For nothing external obscures or influences his freedom. Now, however, it is the nature of joy to want to share itself. What would the long-awaited goal be, when a football team threatened with relegation takes the lead, if one was not allowed to cheer, smile or go and tell everyone about it? It is in the nature of love to want to express itself. What kind of love would it be, that never gave gifts, never complimented, caressed or invited the loved one in? And it is the nature of beauty to want to show itself. Certainly, joy does not force anyone to join in the celebration. Love that compels a kiss is no true love. And even watching the most beautiful sunset, no one can be forced to acknowledge God. God created the world to manifest his glory. God created the world to share in his joy. God chose a people to reveal his whole being to them. Why? Because he is clear that his glory is the most important, the most captivating and praiseworthy thing that exists. Beauty wants to share itself. And from the Garden of Eden to the cross of Christ, from the resurrection to the coming of Jesus in glory, the whole story of God and his people, with all their ups and downs, tells the grand story of what God is like. That he is worth it all. That he made something good, out of nothing. Indeed, that 'He has made everything beautiful in its time' (Ecclesiastes 3:11a). That he really is *echad* and that it is wisdom to trust him in the middle of our darkest of times. This is the meaning of the story of salvation and it is the meaning of the whole Bible in the manifold complexity of its books: it tells of God. It tells of God revealing his glory in creation. How he has revealed his name, his nature and his feelings in his dealings with the people of Israel. Of God, finally, having his own heart torn open, so that we can finally look in. He who descends in all his glory to the mire of Golgotha, into which the blood of the Son of God drips, to announce to the last breath how utterly incomparable this God is. The God, finally, who awakens Jesus from the dead, sends the Holy Spirit and opens to his people a whole new dimension of life, so that through him – wonder of wonders – his own life is imparted to us.

And indeed, this is exactly the focus and the centre of the mission of Jesus. No, he did not just come to show a way to peaceful coexistence. He was no social revolutionary. No ancient Mahatma Gandhi or Jewish version of the Dalai Lama. And no, he is not a religious teacher among many. Anyone who claims this has created a picture of Jesus which the Jesus of the New Testament would not recognize. The message Jesus brought was the Father. What's new is that he revealed God: as he is. However, God is not the content of Jesus' message but, rather, he becomes visible in Jesus himself. 'The Son is the image of the invisible God' (Colossians 1:15), he 'who is himself God and is in the closest relationship with the Father,' and brings news of him (John 1:18b), who announces the name of the Father (John 17:26), and does this through the finger of God (Luke 11:20), who speaks the words of God (John 14:10), and who sees him sees the Father (John 12:45).[26] What was important to Jesus? He was concerned with exactly what God is concerned with, throughout creation and the history of salvation. What was important to Jesus was exactly the same as what was important to God, because he is God. He was concerned with showing what he is like, so that his nature could be made manifest and honoured. That is exactly what it means that the *name* of God – in the Hebrew understanding, name is not only a word, but everything that makes him and

26 When this book speaks of the 'testimony of Scripture' or the 'message of Jesus', ignoring the diversity of biblical books, their historical growth, their literary peculiarities and their different contexts, it is not to appear as if the exploration of the Bible, with modern methods of exegesis, is superfluous or unknown to the author. Scripture is understood rather as a unity in its diversity. As is witnessed in the community of the people of Israel's and the young church's experiences with God. Although written by human hand, certain writings were recognized as inspired by God, according to Christian understanding. All of these writings are themselves in the context of other biblical writings. On the opportunities and limits of critical exegesis, what Hans Urs von Balthasar says has remained valid: 'Let us pay all due respect to historical criticism, including that applied to the New Testament texts: it can help us to see many things more clearly, in better perspective. But one is very quickly confronted with a decision, either to accept the uniform collective witness of the New Testament writings as it is meant – the early church, so successful in mission, did just that – or to question this witness against the background of one's own kind of truth, to split it up into things that are reasonable to the so-called modern person and those which are no longer reasonable.' *New Elucidations*, translated by Sister Mary Theresilde Skerry (Ignatius Press, 1986) (our translation).

what he stands for – is known and sanctified. No wonder, then, that Jesus also teaches us to pray exactly so: in the first part of the Lord's Prayer there is the petition that the name of God be 'hallowed', that is, made holy (Matthew 6:9). In the centre of the story of Jesus and in the centre of the history of God with his people is he himself. He is the message.

All this … for what? God forces no one. He doesn't simply send a decree from heaven and await submission. He doesn't just write a book and then demand obedience.

He tells a story. A big, wide ranging, elaborate story that begins with creation. A creation that springs from his own free will and his own joy. A story that enables a voluntary reaction from those he has created. But he is so concerned about the voluntary nature of worship that he creates a world in which even atheism is possible. In which not even one's mind is 'forced' to acknowledge the Creator. What sometimes irritates the believer and strengthens the unbeliever in his unbelief ('If God really exists, why does he not show himself more clearly then?') can also be interpreted quite differently as deliberate restraint, as leaving some space, a courteous distance. He wants to lure, but not violate. He invites worship and obedience, but he creates a world in which both are neither automatic nor coercive.[27] He places the man in a garden, and the woman with him, where they consciously have the opportunity to eat from a forbidden tree. Why this? To tempt or torment them? But what else could be the meaning of this tree in the midst of countless other wonderful trees? Well, if all trees were allowed, then autonomous disobedience would be impossible. Then they could not help but behave according to the rules of the game. It would be a world without freedom of choice, without options. God and humankind would understand each other wonderfully, but only because his created beings cannot do otherwise. Only where there is a choice, only where there is freedom of choice, is love genuine, is worship genuine, is praise

27 Ulrich Ferdinand, *Atheismus und Menschwerdung* (Einsiedeln, 1966), p.60f.

genuine. And God does not long for applause, but for friends: those who voluntarily agree to honour him. Those who delight in the same things he delights in. He is looking for those who pray to him because they know him. Motivated by joy in him, as God is himself joy.

AND FOR DESSERT – PRAISE

Think of a master chef. For me, this is not hard, because I really like going out to eat and it makes me happy. This chef, a true master of his trade, has developed a series of very special new dishes. He has fortunately had the opportunity to buy some exceptionally rare ingredients and by a lucky coincidence the time was ripe to open some of his best vintage wines. He could cook for himself and drink the wines alone, but this idea seems absurd to him. Cooking for yourself is no fun, he needs guests! That is, he does not need them. There is no real necessity. The food would be the same even without guests. The guests don't 'give' anything to him, neither do they add another star, nor make him richer. But he is a chef and as a chef he loves to inspire people through the art of cooking. Not because he has to, but because it's his way of being hospitable and because he enjoys cooking. For the sheer pleasure of it. And so he invites his four best friends. Finally, he can present his new dishes to an audience. For months he has researched, tasted, tried and composed. Now his new ideas are coming to the table for the first time. Iced Perigord truffle on chickweed jelly with a yuzu emulsion and a beluga macaroon, or something like that. This, anyway, is one of the fourteen courses. And the end is not yet clear. One after the other, new dimensions of taste open up. Bitter and sweet, salty and sour touches alternating, contrasting, harmonious, alienating and tempting. The guests are thrilled, lick their plates, ask for explanations, rub their bellies and commend the wine. The perfect drink for every course. The vintage champagne selection. Finally, Bordeaux, Chateau Petrus 1947, for example. When at last all the courses are served, and also a bottle of dessert wine has been drained, one of the guests starts to thank him. To thank him profusely. The food is quite the most exquisite that he has ever eaten anywhere. It is simply overwhelming. To honour the chef for his abounding generosity and mould-breaking hospitality. No, really, it must be said. Such wines, such delicacies, such a table, such a feast! He practically voices a song of praise to the chef. The chef waves it off: that's so kind, not worth mentioning. Nothing delights his heart more than watching his guests taste and appreciate his cuisine. It was more a gift to himself than to them. It was his pleasure. He was honoured to be allowed to cook for them. Asked whether it was hard to praise the chef so emphatically, the guest looks disconcerted. That was the only possible response to such an evening and the least that could be done. He wished he could have expressed better how wonderful it had all tasted. It was an obligation to him to express this. Yes, his joy would be diminished if he was not allowed to share his experience of this wonderful dinner this evening with his friends and colleagues on the days following. God is the cook. And we are the guests, I would like to suggest, in the hope that the example does not seem irreverent. But it clarifies what God's joy is and the glory of his honour.

In worship, the meaning of creation is fulfilled. God does not have to create anything. Nothing obliges him, he is free. It does not cost anything for the sun to shine, but it is simply its essence. And God is beauty and he is an artist. He is *echad*. It is in his nature to want to share and give himself away. Not because he has to, but because he longs for it. And because he has so many ideas. And because he himself is so glorious. Out of pure joy. And so he creates a creature with the ability to feel the sublime, to perceive beauty and to rejoice in it. God is pleased with God. And because it is his nature to communicate, he wants his glory to be seen and honoured. Just as he rejoiced in his creation on the sixth day of creation, so he gives man – created after his image – the ability to rejoice. The Protestant theologian Gerhard Nebel asks, 'Is not every encounter with the beautiful ... A gift to us or an imposed yes to creation?'[28] And one might well shout out loud, 'Yes, that it is!'

To call beauty 'beautiful' is a necessity for the beholder. To praise the food is no grudging obligation on the part of the guest. Rather, the experience is enhanced by it. What a pity it would be if one were just to enjoy, but were not allowed to show it! And it is just simply this; what Scripture means is that man is created to praise God for his glory (Ephesians 1:12). It is not that a bad-tempered, lightning-casting God squeezes a submissive song of praise from the lips of an enslaved creature before the whip cracks again. A terribly distorted, deeply unbiblical picture! Instead a God who tells his story. Who places the nature of his creation before the sight of people. Who sets out the history of God's people before us. God finally places his own son before us and then says, 'Look!' Which invitation could be more beautiful than learning to see? And then to say: 'You are truly exalted'. You are truly *echad*. And that's why you're being rightly worshipped.' Oh that we could learn to see like that. The speechlessness and the technical reason would fall away from us like dirty rags.

A CORAL LETTER

Simon is his name, and yes he is a Christian. At the opening of his shirt, shining broad and gold, is a large crucifix. There, lying amongst the curly chest hair on the brown skin. His feet bare, he had jumped onto the deck of the small boat and had then hoisted two heavy bottles of compressed air on board. Today we want to go far out. With a roar, the diesel engine starts up and blows a brown cloud into the morning air. Rocking into

28 Our translation of Gerhard Nebel, *Das Ereignis des Schönen* (Klett, 1953), p.149.

motion, our wooden white-painted boat passes a grey cruiser of the Egyptian navy, its gun pointing high in the air. We pass two coloured fishing boats on the left, the dull rumble of the harbour gives way to the cry of the seagulls, and to a fresh sea breeze and open water. At last the sandy shoreline retreats, further and further away.

Yes, he is a Christian and his Muslim colleagues respect this, says Simon, the bearded captain with an anchor tattooed on his forearm. But today is not so much about religion, today we want to dive. A short briefing below deck: we can steer towards this reef and that, and these and these fish can be seen there. What the hand signal should be when one has seen a shark. Well, that's a reassuring prospect! Yes, I'm a novice under water. Hours pass. All around us only the glistening, wide, midday ocean: calm water. Something or other by Thomas Mann on my lap. Suddenly we stop. Definitely here? Nothing but water as far as the eye can see. But here, exactly here is the place. Time to change: wetsuit, flippers, mask, weights around the belt and the heavy bottles on the back. I'm standing on the deck like a clumsy robot. There is not much time, Simon climbs ahead of me and I'm already waddling in the direction of the railing. With a splash I land in the water. The cold of the winter sea permeates even through the neoprene wetsuit. We begin to sink into the blueness of the sea, opening like a primeval vault. We glide past coral and rocks. It takes a while for the bubbles to clear from view and for my eyes to acclimatize. And there, in the half-dark deep, suddenly such wonders! Big fish all around me. With paddling arm movements, we glide through silent catacombs, now surrounded by cold rising from black depths, now lapped by the warm current of the sunlit surface. Between rocks, past jagged rising walls, from the depths back up to the sparkling azure, the bubbling trail of my own air column following behind. Suddenly in front of me on the upper side of the rocks, a bed of colours. A carnival of fish, arranged in groups. I swim right through them. Past yellow fish with black stripes, quite small. Past the even smaller, sparkling grey and red, probably hundreds. Pale and silent, big blue ones pass by, with their wide open eyes. Fish everywhere. Translucent, arrow shaped, thin, completely round, fan shaped and wafting, multicoloured and glittering, brown spiny, fat flattened and those that are so small that you cannot quite recognize them. And all around: coral. Rhythmically swaying tentacles and tassels. Red buttons on silky threads. Greenish threads, resembling brains. Stars and pillows, turrets and palm trees with orange spikes. Wherever my eyes range, just wonders. The astonishment has no end, only at some point the air in my bottle will run out. The meandering moray eels far below me, the transparent jellyfish up above, like a void, but inflating itself like a baroque ballgown, and then sinking like a tangle of laundry. Again and again in endless waves.

I had never seen anything like it before. All this was hidden from the eyes of those standing on the deck of the ship, gazing into the distance. It was as if these treasures had been waiting to be discovered. As if a book had always been on the shelf, only to be opened one day for the intricate artwork sketched on its pages to be admired.

The gentle swell lulls me over the peaceful coral reef community, as a story begins to build in my imagination. Consider the following scene: someone finds a letter lying on his doorstep. On the envelope only his name. He opens it and suddenly he is holding an ornate, hand-painted sheet in his hands. Such a delicate filigree can only have been created with a magnifying glass and the finest of brushes. Ornamental flowery tendrils with gold-leaf figures, evenly entwined ornaments. The recipient is full of wonder and notices that the sheet can be unfolded further. He opens it and finds it to be even more carefully painted within. The work of a master. Months of careful diligence, dedication to accuracy and genius at the same time speak of the beguiling combination of strict precision and delicate forms. Finally, he holds the whole sheet open in his hands: it is covered inside and out by the most amazing of all imaginable figures. A masterpiece! But no accompanying note, no explanation, no sender. Whoever in the world sent him such a letter, it touches him. Why choose me? And what does he want to say to me?

It's just this little story and it's these words that come to my mind as I swim, swim and marvel. There somewhere, far out on the Red Sea. In an oceanic nowhere, at a seemingly arbitrary point. At a point where I dip my head underwater and see, see what I have never previously seen. See what's just there for me at that moment. What nobody else sees now. As if all this had been waiting for me. As if the letter had long been sitting on my doorstep. Hoping that I'll take a look inside. *'Who in the world would write me such a letter?'* Still holding this thought in my head, I squelch back, dripping, across the white wooden planks.

From the handwriting, one recognizes the sender. The painting teaches a lot about the painter. Like a small child secretly discovering a big Christmas present and peeping in to it before the time, I'm sitting there dazed. Thomas Mann stays closed. For inwardly I hold another document in my hands, who the sender was, that is not an indecipherable puzzle. How must God feel when he writes such letters and what does he want to reveal about himself to me?

5

PROMETHEUS

WHERE IS THE CATCH?

A God who is pure beauty and wants nothing more than for people to tune in to the praise of his glory. Makes sense. And it sounds just lovely. But then, doesn't it also sound a little … remote from reality? Is this a theologian trying to paint a picture of a perfect world? Indeed, how are the assertions of the history of mankind as revelation of God to be reconciled with our otherwise known human history? Let's start with nature. Of course there is beauty in nature – order and diversity. However, there is also the horrific: animals that eat one another, viruses that destroy lives, catastrophes that destroy entire regions. What is the revelation of God in this? Or do we look to the salvation story? Isn't the Old Testament just a collection of monstrous tales that are no longer reasonable or rational for today's people? How about the rain of fire on Sodom and Gomorrah, the bloody slaughter in the book of Joshua and the archaic penal laws? Isn't Church history just a succession of crimes 'done in the name of God'? 'God wills it'[29] was the motto embroidered on the flags of the crusaders, and 'God with us' was on the belt buckles of the German soldiers in the

29 *Deus Vult* was a battle cry associated with the Crusades.

Second World War. And now talk of a good God who invites us to dinner and sends a multitude of colourful fish as a love letter? How unworldly can you get, one might think?

After all, isn't there reason enough in anyone's own life to doubt the kindness of a glorious God? Couldn't each and every reader tell of so many situations in the state of the world, and in his or her own life, which make the assertion that everything serves the glorification of God, seem almost offensive? And if so: what kind of God is this supposed to be?! No, to swallow all this and include oneself, confident and saintly, in the ranks of God's devotees requires either a loss of everything we stand for, or the abdication of our intellect.

These objections are significant and mustn't be simply swept under the carpet. Furthermore, they aren't just the objections of a few unbelieving critics. They are objections that everyone encounters. Those who don't know them, or don't want to hear them, probably have quite a naïve faith. The encouraging thing is that even the Bible knows these struggles with God. The searching questions. The doubts. The hesitations. And the complaints. All these have their place in the Bible. Even if many believe the opposite, denying their own irritations or turning off all critical thought, this has never been the tool of choice within the broad stream of Jewish or Christian spirituality and theology. These questions need to be thrashed out with perseverance. It all comes down to this. It comes down to our innermost being.

AGAINST THE TITANS' INSOLENCE

There are things that we humans do not know. And there are things we do not understand. We cannot know the future and we do not understand why terrible things happen. It makes no sense. In our own lives, in the lives of our friends and family members, and in the face of boundless mountains of human suffering, it can strike like the clap of a thunderbolt: it all appears pointless. There is no pattern. It is not the evil that suffer while the good are rewarded. Our sense of justice cries out, our longing for justice rebels: for some, life is all lightness and enjoyment, but for others it contains nothing but tears, pain, humiliation and running away. In Georg Büchner's drama, *Danton's Death*, Danton calls suffering the 'rock of atheism'.[30] The rock on which many a childlike faith has been mercilessly crumbled. And who can judge? No one can understand the suffering of another, no one can know when the cup overflows so much that one is no longer willing to, or one can no longer take it. That one can no longer believe or hope, nor even want to.

This is precisely the question. How do you deal with things that you cannot understand, cannot know, cannot control? You can try to ignore them. You can focus on the beautiful side of life. An exercise that, as you get older and with growing confrontation with the real world, gets closer to what we call repression. And you can raise your eyes to heaven. You can pray, ask, beg and implore – the gods or the one God. You can light candles, make offerings, fast or crawl on your knees up holy mountains. Trying to soften the leaden relentlessness of destiny. To outwit blind fate through its twists and turns.

Or you can push it to one side and dismiss it as a childish concern. 'What hope is there for the hereafter?' This is what sounds in the hearts of some pragmatists. No one has articulated that narrow deciding line, or felt it more deeply than the poets and the philosophers. The ridge upon which every man's heart is set. Sometime between the years 1772 and 1774, and the culmination of the Enlightenment movement, is when Johann Wolfgang von Goethe had Prometheus speak one of his most famous poems:

Cover thy spacious heavens, Zeus,
With clouds of mist,
And like the boy who lops
The thistles' heads,
Disport with oaks and mountain-peaks;

30 Georg Büchner, *Danton's Death, Leonce and Lena, Woyzeck* (Oxford University Press, 2008).

Yet thou must leave
My earth still standing;
My cottage, too, which was not raised by thee;
Leave me my hearth,
Whose kindly glow
By thee is envied.

I know nought poorer
Under the sun, than ye gods!
Ye nourish painfully,
With sacrifices
And votive prayers,
Your majesty;
Ye would e'en starve,
If children and beggars
Were not trusting fools.

While yet not a child,
And ignorant of life,
I turned my wandering gaze
Up toward the sun, as if with him
There were an ear to hear my wailings,
A heart, like mine,
To feel compassion for distress.

Who helped me
Against the Titans' insolence?
Who rescued me from certain death,
From slavery?
Didst thou not do all this thyself,
My sacred glowing heart?
And glowedst, young and good,
Deceived with grateful thanks
To yonder slumbering one?

I honour thee, and why?
Hast thou e'er lightened the sorrows

Of the heavy laden?
Hast thou e'er dried up the tears
Of the anguish-stricken?
Was I not fashioned to be a man
By omnipotent Time,
And by eternal Fate,
Masters of me and thee?

Didst thou e'er fancy
That life I should learn to hate,
And fly to deserts,
Because not all
My blossoming dreams grew ripe?

Here sit I, forming mortals
After my image;
A race resembling me,
To suffer, to weep,
To enjoy, to be glad,
And thee to scorn,
As I![31]

Humankind, the plaything of fate, to be delivered from the 'the Titans' insolence'! Would submissive piety help? No, that is precisely what entrenched the slavery of the people! Prometheus, in Greek mythology, dares to bring to man what should really be reserved for the gods: fire! Chained eternally for his brazenness and brutally punished by Zeus, he becomes a hero[32] and a metaphor for the liberation of man, as Immanuel Kant expressed it, saved 'from his self-incurred immaturity'. Karl Marx will later call religion 'the opium of the people',[33] and thus set the tone that

---

31 *The Works of J. W. von Goethe*, ed. by Nathan Haskell Dole, transations by Sir Walter Scott, Sir Theodore Martin, John Oxenford, Thomas Carlyle and others (Francis A. Niccolls & Co, 1839), pp.210–212.
32 Incidentally, this is how it was for Karl Marx in the preface of his dissertation: 'Prometheus is the most eminent saint and martyr in the philosophical calendar.' Karl Marx, 'The Difference Between the Democritean and Epicurean Philosophy of Nature with an Appendix', *Marx-Engels Collected Works Volume 1* (Progress Publishers, 1902).
33 Marx, *A Contribution to the Critique of Hegel's Philosophy of Right* (1843), translated by Joseph O'Malley (Oxford Universtiy Press, 1970).

further develops in Friedrich Nietzsche's writings: it is precisely the trust in a divine authority that enslaves man, alienates him and leaves him bereft of dignity. Nietzsche allows his Zarathustra to exclaim, 'Remain faithful to the earth!'[34] One should not trust those who speak of heaven: for the kingdom of heaven belongs to little children,[35] and yet then, as mankind matures, he yearns for the kingdom of earth. And there they would rule themselves, with no one over them!

The underlying message in all these theories and demands is one of downright rebellion against an alleged order of the universe, against a heavenly ruler who made man to be truly man. What is worshipped in God is nothing more than what is due to mankind, yet up until now they have not found the courage to claim it, and up until now it has been withheld from them, as is claimed everywhere by the classic critics of religion such as Feuerbach,[36] Marx[37] and Nietzsche?[38] Atheism in the name of humanism is the watchword of the French-Algerian philosopher and Nobel Prize winner for literature, Albert Camus. And what in Goethe's Prometheus still sounded like the overreaching of an awakening modernity, for Camus is an open declaration of war:

> *The rebel defies more than he denies. Originally, at least, he does not suppress God; he merely talks to Him as an equal. But it is not a polite dialogue. It is a polemic animated by the desire to conquer. The slave begins by demanding justice and ends by wanting to wear a crown. He must dominate in his turn. His insurrection against his condition becomes an unlimited campaign against the heavens for the purpose of bringing back a captive king who will first be dethroned and finally condemned to*

34 Friedrich Nietzsche, *Also sprach Zarathustra*, ed. by Andrian Del Caro and Robert Pippin (Cambridge Universtiy Press, 2006), p.6.
35 Matthew 19:14
36 Ludwig Feuerbach, *The Essence of Christianity* (HardPress, 2017).
37 Marx, *Economic and Philosophic*, I,1
38 Nietzsche: WW (edited by K. Schlechta) II, 1159: 'The concept of' God 'was invented as an antithesis to life (...)'. The notion of the 'beyond', 'true world', invented to devalue the only world in existence-to leave no purpose, no reason, no task for our earthly reality.

*death. Human rebellion ends in metaphysical revolution
… When the throne of God is overturned, the rebel realises
that it is now his own responsibility to create the justice,
order, and unity that he sought in vain within his own
condition, and in this way to justify the fall of God. Then
begins the desperate effort to create, at the price of crime
and murder if necessary, the dominion of man. This will
not come about without terrible consequences, of which
we are so far only aware of a few.*[39]

Poets and philosophers have often sensed what all this is really
about. Or, to put it another way, they have expressed what many
of us, especially today, instinctively feel but fail to verbalize:
that God is not tame. That, even with an appealing image, like
that of a master chef, in the end it is about something quite
fundamental. It is about the question of how one reacts to the
absolute and objective. To the Almighty. Can we humbly bow
our heads and trustingly submit? Or is it not, far more, the
screaming command of our autonomy and our self-esteem, to
stand up for ourselves? Would it not be false and cowardly, in
the face of all the blood and tears of the world, to flatter with
incense-wafting the one who is to blame for all this? Is revolt and
opposition not the inevitable demand of humanity and decency?

The Bible takes this question seriously and is not content
with a simple answer. It is a question that goes so far back in
our historical memory, and that pervades human history, that
the Bible puts it in the Creation story, the narrative of origin.
Whether understood literally or symbolically, in the story
of Adam and Eve in the Garden of Eden we encounter such
basic, such fundamental truths about people, that to describe
it as 'merely illustrative' misses the heart of the matter. Are
we to understand it to be historical? Well, if not historical, we
could respond that it is meant to be far more real than merely
historical. It is our story, the story of Adam and Eve. Of man,
humankind – for that's what Adam means. It is the story of
every single person, each and every one of us and the history

---

39 Albert Camus, *The Rebel: An Essay on Man in Revolt,* translated by Anthony Bower (Vintage Books, 1956), p.25.

of humanity as a whole. And it starts with the simple fact that Adam and Eve have no access to a certain tree. How the fruit tastes, they do not know; what it does, they do not know. All they have heard about it is what God has said to them, 'you must not eat from the tree … and you must not touch it, or you will die.' (Genesis 3:3) Nothing about the situation is coincidental. God creates Adam and Eve and deliberately puts them in a situation where there is something they do not know. And in which they either believe his word or choose not to believe it: it is their decision. How the story ends is well known.

Noteworthy, however, is the exact manner with which the seducer makes his approach. He asks if God really said they cannot eat 'from any tree in the garden'. (Genesis 3:1) The fact is that Adam and Eve are allowed to eat from all of the trees, all except one. The image the serpent projects is that of a God who withholds what is really good. A God who doesn't allow something. Whether it's all trees or one tree: either way, he does not permit some things, is sparing with some things; he has his restrictions. At Eve's answer, the deceiver unpacks the actual weapon:

> 'You will not certainly die,' the snake said to the woman. 'For God knows that when you eat from it your eyes will be opened, and you will be like God, knowing good and evil.'
> GENESIS 3:4–5

Significant things are hidden in the nuances. The heart of the matter is that 'God knows much more …' It suggests he does not say everything; he has secrets. He just wants your obedience. But this obedience keeps you small, stupid and inferior. Through obedience you remain ignorant. And the snake's suggestion resonates: if you want to make something of yourself, you have to break with God. You can even be like him! But only on condition that you have to be ready to decide for yourself what is good and evil.

We do not know how Eve felt. But we know what it feels like to be in a similar situation ourselves. It is the situation of not knowing something, nor understanding it. And the situation of simply trusting in a god feels so boring and childish. But we want an explanation. We want to know.

The realization hits Adam and Eve like a blow. For it is different from what they had expected. Immediately after that bite of the forbidden fruit, they realize what they have lost. They did not become wise, but homeless. They see and they know, but this knowledge is a harsh knowledge, one that ruthlessly reveals that they are naked and defenceless.

• •. • •. •°• ● ●. •°•. • • •.

LISBON 1755

The question of obedience and trust in God, and the temptation of rebellion against him, are in every human life. Often articulated only by the poets.

Camus felt it with great clarity: one does not finish with God in passing. To rewrite him as a harmless 'principle of kindness', or a higher being who never intervenes in the world, did not even occur to him. He felt that there are only two possibilities. It's either him or me. Either he is the king and I trust his word, or I become a rebel who declares the ruler a usurper, finally leading him captive to the guillotine. *Écrasez l'infâme!*[40] Either he has the last word or I do, either ego rules or God rules. Real, deadly conflict. Seen more clearly, frankly, by Nietzsche and Camus than by many Christians.

This is a conflict that is not generally an academic one, however it is one that ignites when it comes to suffering. A conflict that man with his sense of reason simply cannot solve. This conflict, according to tradition, was first described by the Greek

---

40 'Shatter the shameful ones!' was Voltaire's battle cry. He meant the Catholic Church. The call was taken up in the French Revolution, which was directed against state and religious power at the same time, and propagated either open atheism or an atheist deism.

philosopher Epicurus: God is either good but not almighty, or omnipotent but not good. The proof: if he's good, he's obviously not all-powerful because the world is obviously full of suffering. On the other hand, if God is all-powerful, he cannot possibly be good. He is then, without a doubt, a cruel or indifferent God, and the suffering in the world either leaves him cold or perhaps even pleases him. Or God is neither good nor powerful. In all three cases God is not worthy of worship, and therefore the idea of God has failed, capsized on the rock of atheism, which is known as suffering. Epicurus' logical consequence: gods live in parallel worlds, do not care about people and therefore are not worthy of worship. People do not need to fear punishment or other divine intervention. And reverence, not at all.

The philosophical discipline that Epicureanism initiated, which deals with the question of God and suffering, is called 'theodicy'. An ambiguous name. It means the justification of God in the face of suffering in the world. While the basic problem has been the same since the beginning of humanity, the first known formulation was described by Gottfried Wilhelm Leibniz (1646–1716). When on 1 November 1755 – All Saints Day – the city of Lisbon is almost completely destroyed by an earthquake, followed by a tsunami and a major fire, the theodicy problem becomes one of the most debated issues among European scholars. Voltaire, Kant, Lessing, Hume, Rousseau: all the great names in the history of eighteenth-century philosophy deal with the question of theodicy. But why this sudden increase in interest? Of course, the Lisbon earthquake is among the greatest natural disasters of European history. But why not a flood of theodicy literature after one of the great plagues of the Middle Ages, after the Thirty Years' War or after the great fire of London in 1666? The catastrophe, along with Leibniz's preoccupation with the question, falls into the phase of the Enlightenment which has been repeatedly critically highlighted in this book. An epoch of intellectual history which, like any other, is accompanied by particular emphasis and also neglect, particular strengths and also weaknesses.

The special emphasis of the Enlightenment is this: the ability of human reason to explain the world; Hegel's quote in the first chapter is an outstanding example. The movement of the '*Encyclopédistes*' tries in the eighteenth century to collect and make available the sum total of human knowledge in existence. Project *Measuring the World,* to adopt the ironic title that Daniel Kehlmann used in his well-known contemporary German novel about the generation of Humboldt and Gauss.[41] The obvious weakness is the lack of a sense of what human reason cannot do. However, it is hardly surprising that the pioneers of such a concept of reason came into conflict with the belief in an almighty, and at the same time trustworthy, God. And so, suddenly, the question of the 'justification of God'. Yes, what actually gives him … the right? And with what authority does he demand faith? On what grounds does one trust him? Can it actually be justified? The line of reasoning is clear. Once human reason has been used as an ultimate authority, it must sit in judgment over everything. If logic and science are on the throne, even the Most High is summoned before the tribunal. Why should God be allowed to escape fair judgment? If one is to continue to believe in him, or if religion is to continue to play a role in the enlightened world, grounds must be given. The desire to be judge, even over good and evil, has not been relinquished since that day in the Garden of Eden. And if one wants to continue to accept an almighty God, he must also be able to identify himself as good. Because simply to trust his words is naïve. 'God knows much more', said the serpent.

Once the rational model of the Enlightenment has finally been established, the theodicy question refuses to be silenced. Leibniz still assumes that God created the best possible world. After 1755, the image of God for the Enlightenment became, more and more, a moral image of a God of deism. A God as the highest principle, according to Kant, was a necessary postulate, but not a God who intervenes in world history. Therefore, there is no one who prevents evil. Liberal theology follows at once and presents a demythologized reading of the gospels. Jesus did not work miracles; God does not influence the course of the world.

41 Daniel Kehlmann, *Measuring the World* (Pantheon: 2006).

In the end, it no longer really matters whether the deistic God really exists anymore or if he is just another name for Hegel's 'World Spirit'. A construct in any case, that Marx and Engels could sweep away with little effort. Such a concept of God really raises no question about theodicy. It was effortlessly dumped and the realm of dialectical materialism was established.

That the conquering triumph of communism did not bless the world, but instead led it into fascism, and indeed, in enlightened, technically developed states, to the nameless horrors of the two World Wars, was what caused thinkers like Horkheimer, Adorno and Hannah Arendt to speak of the 'Dialectic of the Enlightenment', of the fragility of the underlying concept of reason. It is exactly that concept of reason that was presented in the first chapter, as the one in which the island is confused with the globe. In which mankind no longer knows his limit. And yet cannot withstand a spring tide.

THE ROOTS OF MISTRUST AND THE PENDULUM

The more powerful they are, the more pressing the question of whether one can trust them or not.

The foundational experience of every human being is that of being a little child. There are older people who know more and can do more. How should we behave towards them? Can we trust their words? The first people whose motives we do not comprehend and whom we do not quite understand are our own parents or early carers. I should not play with the candle because I will burn my fingers, but the flickering light of the flame is so beautiful to look at and entices me to touch it. Should I really believe the word of my parents, or do they not 'know much more'? Do they know that it's actually a wonderful experience, one that they simply begrudge me?

The first people through whom a child is confronted with omnipotence are their own parents. Whether for good or for evil. What these parents are like will decide how a person learns to think about omnipotence. Is this something I can confidently throw myself into the arms of because I know I'm safe? Because I know that my father and mother know more than I do, but that they are good? Good also where I might imagine otherwise? Does this not describe a trite psychological analysis of the question of God? Anyone with good parents will go on to believe in God, otherwise not. On the one hand, such a statement can hardly be statistically proven, but from the start, it misses the heart of the matter. And every person is confronted with the fundamental fact that authority is not always, and not entirely, trustworthy. There might be not only a breaking of individual basic trust, but also a break in that of the collective history of mankind. This is another word for what theology calls original sin. At least part of it. Something in our basic trust is broken and it has to do with the image that we carry within ourselves regarding authority. And with all the possible images of God that we carry within us. Every time a person refuses to believe in an almighty God who is supposedly good, even though the world is so evil, an echo resounds in him of that first word of suspicion that the serpent placed in Eve's ear.

'Our Father in Heaven' is, however, how Jesus teaches his disciples to address God. God is Father. And God is in heaven. Both aspects are important, both aspects illuminate different things: God the Father, the loving, the close, the caring, the trustworthy. And at the same time, the Father in heaven. Not the earthly, but the otherworldly. Exalted and holy. Transcendent and divine. A god who is only father and only good, but not sovereign and almighty, is harmless.

It seems that these two aspects, 'Father' and 'Heaven', signify two poles in the arc of a pendulum.[42] The further the pendulum swings in one direction, the further it swings in the other. A God who cannot threaten me, because he is never incomprehensible, may be a friendly acquaintance, but not a father. Or just a weak father, one who barely concerns me. The image of a God who

---

42 I am indebted to Timothy Keller for this comparison, like many other suggestions for this chapter. On the theme of theodicy, Timothy Keller's *Walking with God through Pain and Suffering* (Hodder & Stoughton, 2015) is highly readable and practical.

has nothing to do with the evil in the world, because he is as sorry as we are about it. Who perhaps also suffers with us, or is even reliant on our help. But certainly not one who expects us to believe that he holds everything in his hands. Or that he knows what he is doing and that this world that we see, so broken, is what he actually wants. Surely not one who has such plans, of which we have no comprehension. Whose intentions are hidden and exalted, so that we have no discernment whatsoever. And that cannot even be marred by the undeniable existence of suffering, injustice and death.

With such a swing of the pendulum, one cannot believe in a god who allows judgment or even hell. The nice kind god of the gentle Jesus, who has nothing to do with the warlike god of the Old Testament. A god who does not expect me to act in faith, who does not demand a decision from me, but who only shines on the horizon as a silent star. Such a god does not challenge me, and neither does he radiate any strength in which I could take refuge.

A father who is weak can certainly not punish me. But he cannot protect me either. He cannot throw me in the air and catch me again. He cannot surprise me. The pendulum swings in both directions, of necessity. The biblical God has never held out the option of being able to be reinterpreted as a deistic God who has to explain himself before the mind of mortal man. He never offers to be just our friend. He is and always will be the Father in heaven: the near and consoling, who is at the same time the sovereign ruler of the universe, who does not owe an account of his ways to anyone.

And yet it can cost everything to find this Father.

JOB'S MESSAGE

The Bible does not offer quick, shallow reassurances; it allows for doubting and wrestling. Nowhere is this clearer than in the book of Job. Conflict is not resolved here in a straightforward way.

There's a God-fearing man named Job. He lives an exemplary and happy life. Until one day, according to the story, he is put to the test by the devil to prove whether he is so devout only because he is doing so well. A little experience of suffering and he will soon curse God to his face, according to the devil (Job 1:11). God is convinced of the contrary and allows the tempter to proceed. What follows is the proverbial bad news. Within a very short time, Job sees himself exposed to every imaginable human tragedy. The robbery of his possessions, the death of his children, the loss of his health: so far, the details of the story are familiar.

It is less well understood, however, that the vast majority of the book of Job deals not directly with Job's misfortune or happiness, but with the attempts by pious friends to interpret the event theologically. Chapter by chapter, Eliphaz the Temanite, Bildad the Shuhite and Zophar the Naamathite propose their arguments of theodicy. Every one of them voices explanations that you would expect. That God knows what he is doing. That it all eventually ends well for the righteous. That one can learn so much through suffering. Maybe Job was also partly guilty? All those well-intentioned words that are easy to say, for people who have not suffered very much themselves. Attempts at explanations that hurt people more than they help them. Job cannot be comforted by all this. If he initially agreed with God's hidden counsel, his disagreements become ever clearer. He was innocent and did not deserve God's punishment.

> 'As surely as God lives, who has denied me justice,
>   the Almighty, who has made my life bitter,
> as long as I have life within me,
>   the breath of God in my nostrils,
> my lips will not say anything wicked,
>   and my tongue will not utter lies.
> I will never admit you are in the right;
>   till I die, I will not deny my integrity.
> I will maintain my innocence and never let go of it;
>   my conscience will not reproach me as long as I live.'
> JOB 27:2–6

Weighty words! Is this the totally submissive servant, the plaything of the Titans? The self-confidence with which Job is confronting God and standing up for his rights would be almost worthy of Prometheus, it almost sounds like the 'man in revolt'. But now: does God hold with such bold questions? Is such heckling allowed? Or are the theologizing friends right when they claim from the beginning to know the correct answer?

Triple wonder. Firstly, that this story and the words of Job are in the Bible at all. Forty-two chapters long, one of the longest books in the Bible. It appears to be an important topic, a legitimate topic. One that cannot be dealt with in just a few verses. And in this Job has doubts, complaints and struggles and gets to express them to an audience.

Secondly: Job's speeches are expressly not blamed. That is the case in everything he says, 'In all this, Job did not sin in what he said'. (Job 2:10) God can handle this. It is allowed. It may take time and it is normal that it is painful.[43]

Thirdly: when God begins to speak for himself at the end of the story, it is the friends who are blamed, not Job. God apparently had no pleasure in the theological head knowledge and the standard answers. In fact, God's wrath was firstly on these religious geeks, and they needed Job to intercede for them!

Most interesting, however, is how the story of Job ends. What will be God's reaction to Job's suffering and his complaint? What answer will he give? How is suffering mitigated? The passage is of such force and poetry that it is here word for word:

> *Then the LORD spoke to Job out of the storm. He said:*
> *'Who is this that obscures my plans*
> *with words without knowledge?*
> *Brace yourself like a man;*
> *I will question you,*
> *and you shall answer me.*

---

43 For more on the justification of the lawsuit and the meaning of mourning, see Johannes Hartl, *Wenn die Seele weint* (Haiterbach-Beihingen, 2014).

'Where were you when I laid the earth's foundation?
  Tell me, if you understand.
Who marked off its dimensions? Surely you know!
  Who stretched a measuring line across it?
On what were its footings set,
  or who laid its cornerstone –
while the morning stars sang together
  and all the angels shouted for joy?

'Who shut up the sea behind doors
  when it burst forth from the womb,
when I made the clouds its garment
  and wrapped it in thick darkness,
when I fixed limits for it
  and set its doors and bars in place,
when I said, "This far you may come and no farther;
  here is where your proud waves halt"'?
JOB 38:1–11

And there follows an enumeration of the wonders of creation. This includes a listing of all the aspects of nature about which man has no idea. Special attention is given to some animals, including the crocodile (Leviathan) and the hippopotamus (Behemoth).[44] The crocodile and the hippopotamus in response to the question of theodicy? Apparently so! Both animals are wild, highly dangerous to humans. They cannot be tamed. And in the speech of God from the storm, Job encounters the wild, the enigmatic and the untamed side of God.

'Can you pull in Leviathan with a fishhook
  or tie down its tongue with a rope?
Can you put a cord through its nose
  or pierce its jaw with a hook?
Will it keep begging you for mercy?
  Will it speak to you with gentle words?'
JOB 41:1–3

44 In most English translations of the Bible, Leviathan and Behemoth are not translated. The translations 'crocodile' and 'hippopotamus' are unusual, but not without grounds.

The answer is of course: no. There are even aspects of nature that we humans cannot understand and certainly cannot tame. How much less the counsels of God! But this realization is one Job could not have come to from a book. He could not have been told it by any of his friends. What solved the riddle for him was an encounter with God. And this was only at the end of the painful process of suffering, questioning, doubting and praying. And so Job's reaction is not only a rational insight into the systematics of theodicy, but an act of humility, a bow. Of course a bow, but not because he is defeated, but in that he must give way. The voluntary submission to a God whom he now knows personally:

> 'My ears had heard of you
>   but now my eyes have seen you.
> Therefore I despise myself
>   and repent in dust and ashes.'
> JOB 42:5–6

So what is the solution to the theodicy question according to Job? It is not rational, but experiential; and it is not an intellectual appraisal, as this is exactly what usually fails, but it is an encounter with God. An encounter with a God who, contrary to what one might expect, does not show himself as comforting and merciful, but as the glorious one. It is precisely the confrontation with the sovereignty of the Creator, whose ways are far superior, that tore Job out of his fixation on his own suffering. And he chooses to worship. An act of worship, however, that does not humiliate but liberates. It is the majestic side of God himself that lifts Job out of himself, out of endlessly thinking about himself, and lets him breathe again.

THE 24

Yes, it costs Job a great deal to acknowledge God. We know that God blesses Job's later days more than his earlier ones, and that in the book all ends well. But he does not know that at the moment of surrender. And yes, it's a surrender; a recantation; a denial. The admission that his suspicions against God were wrong. And that God is not unfair just because he does not fit in with the categories of human thought. Such a step has nothing to do with self-destruction, but rather with an inner act of which the last book of the Bible speaks of in an impressive scene:

At once I was in the Spirit, and there before me was a throne in heaven with someone sitting on it. And the one who sat there had the appearance of jasper and ruby. A rainbow that shone like an emerald encircled the throne. Surrounding the throne were twenty-four other thrones, and seated on them were twenty-four elders. They were dressed in white and had crowns of gold on their heads. From the throne came flashes of lightning, rumblings and peals of thunder. In front of the throne, seven lamps were blazing. These are the seven spirits of God. Also in front of the throne there was what looked like a sea of glass, clear as crystal.

In the centre, round the throne, were four living creatures, and they were covered with eyes, in front and behind. The first living creature was like a lion, the second was like an ox, the third had a face like a man, the fourth was like a flying eagle. Each of the four living creatures had six wings and was covered with eyes all round, even under its wings. Day and night they never stop saying:

"'Holy, holy, holy
is the Lord God Almighty,"
who was, and is, and is to come.'

Whenever the living creatures give glory, honour and thanks to him who sits on the throne and who lives for ever and ever, the twenty-four elders fall down before him who sits on the throne and worship him who lives for ever and ever. They lay their crowns before the throne and say:
'You are worthy, our Lord and God,

> *to receive glory and honour and power,*
> *for you created all things,*
>   *and by your will they were created*
>   *and have their being.'*
> REVELATION 4:2–11

Before the throne of God are twenty-four people, clearly human. 'Twenty-four' as the doubling of the biblical number twelve: sum of the number of tribes of Israel and the twelve apostles. The sum of redeemed humanity, representative of the people of God. It is interesting that God's greatness does not depend on the fact that no one can exist in his presence, that before him all have to crawl into the dust. Rather, his creatures sit before him, upright, on thrones and crowned. Already in the Old Testament, in Psalm 8, the concept of God crowning man is declared![45] To speak of man as the slave of God, at the mercy of the King's word, is unworthy of the biblical God.

Now something interesting happens. Around God's throne, there are angels singing, day and night. Without external coercion and quite spontaneously, the twenty-four are overcome with praise and prostate themselves. They lay their golden crowns at his feet. A deep gesture, impressively interpreted by Romano Guardini. The crown symbolizes one's own dignity, one's own sphere of influence. The removal of the crowns is not a renunciation of autonomy and responsibility, instead it is a voluntary act on the part of the created. Of our own free will, we recognize that we are facing someone beside whom our own importance is irrelevant. Before whom it is best if the ego quickly gets off the throne.

The reason immediately follows, 'For you are the one who created the world' – it could be put like this: in the end, all my honour, my dignity and every fibre of my being I owe to you. You are the source from which everything comes. My crown belongs to me, it will not be taken from me, but I lay it at your feet.

It is not until the sight of the sacrificed Lamb in Chapter 5

---

45 Psalm 8:5.

of the Revelation of John that all creatures unanimously join in the praise. The Lamb and the Lion, that's what Jesus Christ is called in the last book of the Bible. The Lion: the majestic, mighty and ruling side of God. And the Lamb: Jesus, God who became man, who gave himself out of love and did not resist, to the death. Being pierced because of our sins. Who was wrongly convicted, but did not defend himself. He drank the cup of suffering to the dregs. Misunderstood, convicted as a criminal, mocked, beaten, tortured, put to death outside the city in the bloodiest of ways. All this without any guilt, without sin and pure as a white lamb. And right in front of the throne, in the midst of the royal glory of the heavenly court, this Lamb suddenly stands. A pierced, sacrificed Lamb. And now the choir swells, everyone is now singing along, this is the moment when everything is understood:

Then I heard every creature in heaven and on earth and under the earth and on the sea, and all that is in them, saying:

> *'To him who sits on the throne and to the Lamb*
> *be praise and honour and glory and power,*
> *for ever and ever!'*
> REVELATION 5:13

These passages from Revelation seek to demonstrate that, yes, God is the holy one. He is majestic, but his majesty is not deaf to suffering. He himself suffered, he took sin on himself, he experienced meaninglessness and suffering inflicted on his own body. An experience more cruel than anyone else has suffered. And from that day, the dying, the suffering and the sick have inexplicably found comfort in looking at a wooden crucifix. A strange comfort, because the sight of the Crucified One answers no questions. It provides no head knowledge. It explains as little as the encounter with God in the storm that afflicted Job. Yet it resolves every question. The sight of the sacrificed Lamb is an invitation: look, my heart is open. I cannot explain everything to you now; there is much you cannot understand now. It is only at the end of history, and from the perspective of heaven, that all created beings, no matter what suffering they have experienced, confess: you are worthy of sitting on the throne. But until then no one can be released from the need for acting in faith. Whether God is truly trustworthy, or whether he actually withholds the best fruits and the most beautiful trees when we let him be God, we have to find out for ourselves. And yet, a way now stands open for us. The way home.

The great atheist and religious critic Friedrich Nietzsche wrote in 1884:

Shrill shriek the crows
that to the town in whirls roam:
soon come the snows –
weal unto him, who - has a home!

Now you stand still,
look back, alas! how far unfurled!
You fool! You will
escape the winter to the world?

The world – a gate
to thousand deserts, mute and chill!
Who lost his fate,
as you have lost, stands nowhere still.

Now you are pale
and cursed to wander winter's rise,
like fumes prevail
that always seek the colder skies.

Seek, bird, and shriek
your desert-bird-song, worn and torn! –
And hide, you freak,
your bleeding heart in ice and scorn!

Shrill shriek the crows
that to the town in whirls roam:
soon come the snows –
woe unto him, who has no home![46]

We find ourselves in these images. The price for man not being willing to trust, and making his mind the measure of all things, is the loss of home and the expulsion from paradise. Yet for how much longer?

It seems as if we are being called: Come on, Prometheus, let us reconcile. Give up your rebellion, which has only made you harder, poorer and more naked. The great revolution that, indeed, again and again, has broken all its promises, and yet has still devoured its own children. The dream of the human kingdom, which leaves people ever more enslaved than they had been before. Come home and meet with the Father. Let yourself be taken by the hand. On the cross you can see what the rebellion did. But on the cross, you also see what price the Father pays to ransom you. To bring you home. It is time to return. And time to lay down your crown.

THE DAY WHEN MY BEST FRIEND DIED

Once again, I am sitting by the sea. Under the unbelievably blue sky of Cyprus. As if it is noon all day long. The sun is apparently at home here and makes only occasional courtesy visits to countries beyond the Alps. Somewhere beyond the Alps and infinitely far away, it all feels like home. Maybe also, because

46 Friedrich Nietzsche, *The Complete Works of Friedrich Nietzsche, Vol 15: Unpublished Fragments from the Period of* Thus Spoke Zarathustra *(Spring 1884–Winter 1884/85)*. This book is due to be published by Stanford University Press, but it not currently available in English. This poem is our translation of the original German. Nietzsche himself, of course, conceived the 'free spirit' as a dialogue poem. The complaint is followed by an answer in which the longing for home is given a harsh rejection. Perhaps the atheist author has simply felt both sides in himself: the inner homelessness on the one hand and the firm determination to no longer want to give up his religion-free autonomy? In any case, he deeply felt the weight of this decision and its price.

everything at home is no longer now how it once was. Because one can't imagine what it was actually like anymore. Back then, when everything was still the same as always. Back then, in that irretrievable yesterday gone by, that lies so galactically distant, even though it was only a few weeks ago. With a heavy heart, how do you sit on a sunny beach? On a tray of glistening light, with a shadow on your soul. Breaking into a thousand fragments of gold on the sparkling sea, even there, at the corner of my eye, where the view is blurred. Breaking into tears, which rise up my nose bitterly, and then expand, like a dense veil. This inner flood, which comes again and again after each ebb, even if these episodes eventually become less frequent.

It was a Tuesday in August when my best friend died. And with him a part of me. A world has died – one that since then only exists in my memories. A world in which as teenagers we had spent whole nights out and had gone searching for girls. Not always the most glorious memories. Climbing into someone's car and driving just anywhere. He went to India, I went to Syria, and afterwards we could not stop talking about it, all night long. Through the West Bank, climbing Mount Athos, exploring stalactite caves in the Piedmont, visiting the Romanian Carpathians, Amsterdam and Atlanta. And when I had a high fever, he and Django helped me up that steep mountainside somewhere in northern Israel and carried my kit. Together we prayed, together we pilgrimaged, together we experienced miracles and together we cried, fought and believed. You came from the same place as me, were almost the same age as me, and sometimes we were taken for brothers. We were more than that. And now you are dead.

A day when you did not come. You did not pick up. A few friends went to call on you. I stand in the garden and the world stops turning. Yes, how do you stand in a garden buzzing with bees on a hot August day and find out on the mobile phone that a thirty-seven-year-old, healthy man is dead in his bathroom, a small pool of blood on his face? And this man my most long-standing friend?

My friend Tom left behind a pregnant wife and a three-year-old son. Nobody really knows what he died of. An allergic shock? Does it really matter? I am a person who believes in miracles and has seen many. But his skin is cold when I put my hand on him one last time, two days later in the pathology department.

When this happens to someone, for them, life falls apart. And I was just the friend; what about the wife, the son, the parents, the brother? Do I actually have anything to say?

It is, surprisingly, less a struggle with God or anger that is felt afterwards. Tom was one of the founders of our House of Prayer. A bunch of young people who created a place where prayer does not stop, day or night. How then do such people deal with death? I do not really know. But it is primarily a sense of seriousness, of awe and deep sadness that will shape the coming weeks of summer.

It's strange to be in Cyprus now. I would have imagined the atmosphere in the meeting to be quite different. No, this is no normal holiday. It is a meeting of Christians. Christians from the Middle East. There are houses of prayer, like ours in Augsburg, all over the world. There are even some in the Middle East, mostly under cover. The leaders of these houses of prayer are meeting together, but not in the Middle East, because in most of their countries it would not be safe for them. That's why Cyprus. Among them: my wife Jutta and I.

What these people have been experiencing in the last few weeks cannot really be compared to what we have been through, can it? It is the summer of 2014 and terrorists of the 'Islamic State' have just overrun Mosul. It does not look all that rosy in other countries, either. Things I hear by the buffet, or in the corridor, hit me like a head-on collision with a freight train. We are splashing in the waves when Sharif from Egypt tells me how it was, last year, when the churches were torched. When angry mobs, instigated by the Muslim Brotherhood, were throwing stones at Christians. Yes, it is true that many Muslims converted to Jesus. Many of them then went back to their families and villages to share their faith, true missionaries. Until they were eventually killed. How can one be standing here in the foaming surf in Cyprus, with a heart that can hardly comprehend what it hears? Bernadette and her family lived in Tripoli for a long time, the city in northern Lebanon – I remember my trip there, and a special, sumptuous breakfast with lots of za'atar and goats' cheese. They were the only missionaries there. A young man who had converted to Christianity had lived with her. They were not at home when the bomb exploded, tearing apart her front yard and the ground floor of her house. The young man was dead, but Bernadette did not leave Lebanon, nevertheless.

The young family from the United States, who were providing humanitarian aid in northern Iraq. Who simply remained, with their two small children, even though ISIS was only a few kilometres away. Is that something crazy or am I just not understanding it? We are sitting together by the pool and the situation is way too bizarre for my brain. He talks about expelled Kurds, artillery shells and the fact that they urgently need some container loads of Pampers.

With pain in my heart, I suddenly find myself surrounded by people who have come from places of persecution, terror and constant killing. What did I expect? Well, not easy days, anyway. Even in Germany, the horrors of Syria and Iraq, the Sinjar Mountains and Kobanî flicker on the TV every day. On social networks everywhere there are videos of executions and streams of blood from throats that have been cut. When I had agreed to come to Cyprus as the representative of the European houses of prayer, I had expected to look into a heart of need. I had expected sorrow and distress. But instead I found praise. There is nothing to gloss over here. The situations reported by the Christian leaders, missionaries and pastors are frightening. But there was none of the reaction of horror that I had noted in Europe during the whole gathering. It was deeply moving for me to see how these people prayed and sang songs of praise, not as mere victims.

'For everyone born of God overcomes the world. This is the victory that has overcome the world, even our faith.' (1 John 5:4) I could see evidence of this here. It was not a clumsy optimism, not an our-loving-God-will-make-everything-alright-bless-you. It was the simple fact that these people were used to living with one foot in eternity. It was not news to them that believing in Jesus Christ could cost them their lives – they were constantly confronted with this fact. But far from being downhearted, I saw in the bright young Arab faces a testimony to a dimension of life that was simply greater than the visible. With hands raised, lost in praise. Their songs: 'Lord you are worthy!' Worthy to be loved and followed, even unto death.

° ° . ° ° .° .°° • •.°° °. ° ° ° .

It was a peculiar mix of emotions that went through me when we were finally seated back on the plane. Next to us, white columns of cloud loomed like oversized towers, reminding me of the plague memorial towers of my homeland. And far below, the Cypriot sea, like hammered sheet metal. Everything seemed a little smaller from up here. How big and significant a mountain seems when the winding mountain road causes the engine to groan and the coolant to boil. But from up here, they are only curvy ochre lines on grey-green mounds.

No, the pain was not gone; the mourning for our deceased friend had really just begun. Mourning takes time and that is allowed. And yet the days with the Christians of the persecuted church were more instructive in this situation than any book could have been. They were confronting the greater reality. With the sea surrounding the island. With a horizon that enables you to breathe again and to look up, even if it does not dry the tears, in which the light separates into colours.

6

TREMENDUM

God, not as our buddy, our pal, but rather as Sacred and Wholly Other. No false egalitarianism, but a deep fear of God as the beginning of wisdom, and the realization that it appears to be time to face this God as he is. And thereby not avoiding or suppressing those aspects that are unpleasant to us and monstrous to the ego. The German theologian Rudolf Otto called the sacred, '*Fascinosum et tremendum*'. That which fascinates, but also makes us tremble. It is about God's holiness, about his eternity and omnipotence.

THE ONLY TRUTH ABOUT GOD?

Yet who is God? Who could even claim to know? If God does exist, can 'knowing' God even be possible? And if possible, can it be articulated? And if so, can there be something approaching a 'correct' description of God, or does everyone have their own version?

From Lessing's 'Parable of the Ring' in the play *Nathan the Wise*, most students from German high schools know the alleged principle of tolerance between religions: which of the three great monotheistic religions is really right, no one can say, because each one of the three people in the famous parable has only one copy of the original ring.

Just as widely used is a modern parable, said to be either Indian or Jewish, 'The blind men and the elephant'. The blind person who feels the trunk calls the elephant tubular. The one at its belly insists it is big and round. The one feeling the ears recognizes it as being thin and flexible. And each defends their view of things, and accuses the others of being wrong. The point is easy to grasp. God is the elephant, and so this didactic riddle unfolds. Anyone who claims otherwise does not realize that he is confusing his own perspective with objective truth. All religions are partly right and partly not.

So far so good, and there are some important arguments in support of such a view of God. They might run as follows:

1. The different perspectives of human knowledge. If you ask ten witnesses about an accident, you will hear several different stories. The further the experience moves away from the clearly physical, the greater will be the differences in presentation. A complex family dispute will be presented in many different ways, and the first step in healing would be to admit that there is not only one true version. How much more should one assume that to some extent everyone has his own truth, with something as supernatural as a religious belief.

2. The fact is that a multitude of religions claim to proclaim the only truth about God. So why should only one of them be believed? Isn't the inconsistency between religions the clearest proof that no one can know about God?

3. The history of religion in general, and monotheistic religions in particular, is a history of religious wars, inquisitions and heresy. Can we not say a final farewell to the belief in 'the one truth' and thereby prevent people from being murdered or tortured for their religious affiliation?

To the second argument first. From the fact that the different religions are contradictory, one can only conclude that this is a topic that clearly has very different approaches and which many people think about. For every topic for which this is true, one should assume a difference of opinion. In fact, diversity is likely to increase, the more deeply-held the concerns that are affected. But whether all these opinions are wrong is by no means positively proven. In fact, the question of God and of the transcendent is such a fundamental question of humanity that no one should be surprised that there are also a large number of competing answers. Especially if there really is one true faith, we would certainly expect that there must be many other religions which seem close to it but which do not quite agree with it. The much more important question, of course, is: why exactly should I believe this one teaching about God?

Now to the first argument. In fact, human knowledge – at least broadly speaking – is more perspective and less objective, more so than we might like to admit. Faith in God in the sense of the great monotheistic religions, however, is not just an opinion or a scientific insight about God, but the answer to a revelation. And while there were and are, of course, an infinite number of human traditions and teachings about a higher being, the question arises as to whether a revelation actually occurred. The theologian Hans-Urs von Balthasar says:

> *The divine sense, offered from afar, to learn to be silent before him and to let him prevail: his people may be allowed to reach their frontier; such an anticipation seems to them revelation enough: they discover on the shore of their finiteness something totally different, and as the sea of mystery surrounds, you learn something like piety, a reverence for the unimaginable meaning, which even governs the seemingly senselessness of its existence. ...*
>
> *But supposing that these pious people try to advance humanity to the realm of the unknowable, would they be pushed aside by a counter movement in which the*

abyss and ocean impose on humanity the full reality of
themselves, to expose themselves as 'that' to reveal what
they 'are': if this could happen, how will it happen?[47]

That it happened, that is the testimony of Christianity. Whether
it is to be believed will depend on the credibility of the person
or persons claiming to be witnesses to this revelation. In the
case of Christianity, this means that believing the Christian
message of God stands and falls with the credibility of the
man Jesus. Did he really live? Is the New Testament account
about him reliable? Did Jesus really rise from the dead? The
questions point back to those who wrote the New Testament.
Are the witnesses of the early church reliable? If they were not
convinced of the truth, what led them to be witnesses of the
resurrection of Jesus from the dead, given that this testimony
threatened most of them with a life of persecution and finally a
cruel death? Would you have agreed to go and die for something
that you knew yourself to have been a lie?

Finally, if the historicity of Jesus of Nazareth cannot be denied,
and that it is a premise that is well-established scientifically, how
do we relate to his claim to offer the sole necessary access to
God? 'I am the way and the truth and the life. No one comes
to the Father except through me.' (John 14:6) In the encounter
with the life and the words of Jesus, we are faced with a choice:
is this a work of pious imagination, a malicious lie or simply the
truth? Whether Jesus actually rose from the dead and his grave
was empty is as little dependent on perspective as is the assertion
as to whether he really said that he was the door and whoever
would be saved would gain access through him (John 10:9).

If Jesus lived and worked miracles, if he claimed to act with
divine authority, if he died and rose again, then a revelation
occurred. Even where this revelation occurred in an encounter
with people, which they then passed on in their own words and
with their own emphases, the message itself is not one of many
opinions. It is not an opinion at all: it is God's Gospel, which
means a message from the Lord of the Universe himself.

47 Balthasar, *Herrlichkeit* III/2, Bd. 1, 31 (our translation).

Finally, the third objection: doesn't monotheism necessarily lead to violence? At first glance, this statement sounds very plausible. On closer inspection, however, it can be said once again that wars are and will be waged over anything that is of deep importance to people. Over resources, honour, territory, power and even love. From the fact that wars are waged over a particular thing, we can deduce nothing. More than a few wars of the twentieth century were fought for a particular political model. Is it to be deduced from this fact that democracy, communism and theocracy are all equally good and equally bad?

The question that will be asked in the end is, who do we believe in? Who do we trust to give us information about God? And here, all the parables, like that of the three rings and that of the blind men and the elephant, reveal: none of the persons involved grasp the whole truth. Does that mean that there is no one who comprehends the whole truth? Indeed, there is one: the narrator. Nathan the Wise knows that in reality, there is another ring. The narrator of the elephant story knows that it is really an elephant. Were it not for the narrator's position the various perspectives would have to stand side by side without comment, without anyone even daring to declare all statements to be equally valid. For this statement itself has already become a dogmatic one. Whoever asserts all religions as partial truths has positioned his own interpretation as objective truth. Relativism still defeats itself most impressively: the sentence 'all statements about God are relative' is either – because it applies here! – in itself only relatively true, or simply meaningless.

Do we have to measure ourselves, in order to survey the elephant? Or do we listen to the voice of the only one whose claim to be the Word of God is legitimized by the historical resurrection? In any case, this book is all about the God of Jesus Christ. He is the God of the Bible and the God of church doctrine. And he is, according to Christian understanding, the only true God.

UNAUTHORISED ON HOLY GROUND

'*Ki atah kadosh veshimcha kadosh, k'doshim kol yom yehalelucha, Selah*' the resounding chant sounds over the forecourt to the Wailing Wall. It is the time of morning prayer, and this phrase, from the well-known Jewish prayer of the eighteen blessings, dating from the first century, is being sung: 'You are holy, and your name is holy and those who are holy praise you'. Those who are holy, and with whom I now find myself this morning, consist of a hoarse men's group in the morning heat of Jerusalem. Black smocks, fuzzy beards, the wild swaying of the upper body to the loud-lamenting recitation of the psalms. On the lectern, a pile of holy books. The figures around me resemble robust figures from somewhere between an Eastern European Jewish quarter of the eighteenth century and the tent settlement of a biblical patriarch. I had got myself into this quite by accident. I had been standing, a little undecided, in the vicinity. Then somehow a loose circle of men, praying around a lectern, opened up and suddenly I was standing in the middle of them. How exactly had this happened? A *kippah* on my head and yes, a Hebrew Bible under my arm, but otherwise you might have noticed that I actually did not belong. Hundreds of voices around me singing, mumbling and calling in the ancient language of Israel. I notice the little stooping figure, very close to the side next to me, only when he has already grabbed my hand. Waves of curled side locks, black hat and coat. Eyebrows suitable for Father Abraham himself. The old rabbi seems to think, 'Here is someone who needs a little guidance'. From his pocket he brings out a length of braided leather.

A little roughly and chattering incomprehensibly, he starts with some quick movements and ties the strip around my arm. It is the *tefillin*, the boxes that devout Jews tie on the forehead and upper arm for prayer. The experienced hand movements of a sacred act that has become second nature. An act in which I quite abruptly find myself participating. Suddenly it dawns on me: what if he learns that I'm not a Jew at all? That I had prayed because, as a Christian, I felt close to the people of God's first covenant?

But actually I am not one of them? Something threatening radiates from the old man, from the piercing black of his eyes. A fit of anger from him, would, I imagine, be quite impressive, but by now it's too late anyway. The old man soon finishes and presses the *siddur*, the Jewish prayer book, on me, opened at the page with the prayer that you have to pray when you put on the *tefillin*. With an authoritative gesture, he signals to me that I should pray now. There I stand, my arm so tightly wrapped that I feel blood pulsating along it. Just above my eyes, the big black capsule with the sacred words in it. Here I stand 'within a circle of the holy', just a few steps away from the Western Wall of the Temple, the holiest place in the world for a believing Jew. Incorporated into the millennia-old dynasty of those who wore just such *tefillin* and spoke just such words. The mysterious black characters in the book with the gilt edging dance before my eyes. These letters have survived aeons. In my mind I feel as if I am standing in the forecourt of Solomon's Temple, in a holy place. And under the scrutiny of my newly acquired prayer companions, I suddenly feel like someone who has swum too far out to sea. In a fleeting moment I become aware of how far I am from the safety of shore. Of course, there is no need to worry about my life. However, this feeling of entering a forbidden sanctuary and finding myself unauthorized on sacred ground brings a combination of terror and amazing joy.

This time fate was gracious. The rabbi had handed me a *siddur* with English notes. Therein were guidelines: at which Hebrew words the *tefillin* are to be kissed. With a benevolent look from those Old Testament eyes as they meet mine when I finish praying, I am freed from the strips of leather. He asks my name, and that of my father. Suddenly his hand slides under the strand of hair that covers my forehead. Even these names do not betray my pagan roots. 'I bless you, Johanan, son of Michael, with the blessing of Israel,' (or something similar) whispers the deep voice. Trembling a bit, I go to the exit and feel just so lucky. Somehow I had met with the sacred, and, although undeserving, it had not rejected me; I had been accepted and received.

GOD IS NOT ARBITRARY, BUT HOLY

There is no other adjective throughout the entire Bible that is used as often for God, as this: 'God is holy'. 'There is no one holy like the LORD', (1 Samuel 2:2a). He is the 'Holy One of Israel' (Isaiah 12:6). And the angels around his throne call by day and by night: 'Holy, holy, holy.' (Revelation 4:8) But what does holy mean? In addition to statements about God's holiness, Scripture also knows sacred places and objects:

> *Moses said to the LORD, 'The people cannot come up Mount Sinai, because you yourself warned us, "Put limits around the mountain and set it apart as holy."'*
> EXODUS 19:23

The reason for this is easily found. It was due to the divine manifestation and presence on Sinai, and far from being romantic:

> *Mount Sinai was covered with smoke, because the LORD descended on it in fire. The smoke billowed up from it like smoke from a furnace, and the whole mountain trembled violently. As the sound of the trumpet grew louder and louder, Moses spoke and the voice of God answered him.*
> EXODUS 19:18–19

The place of the sacred is no longer the terrain of man that he can freely enter. He is no longer at home there. Smoke, fire and thunder: it is a place of awe and fear. An uninvited entry risks death. The sanctity of the mountain means that not everyone can ascend safely.

Another aspect in the Old Testament is the meat that is sacred: only a priest may eat of it (Exodus 29:33). Certain oil and incense mixtures may be used only in worship (Exodus 30:31–38). The temple compound is sacred and even contains the Holy of Holies: access is strictly regulated (Exodus 28:35). What is sacred about a mountain, meat, oil, frankincense and a particular room? All this is separated, or set aside, for God. And indeed, this is the underlying semantic root of the Hebrew word for holy, *kadosh*: separate. There is an area that is taboo, it is surrounded by a border, invisible or visible. It is in a different category, one that is for God alone.

What does the statement mean, God is holy? It means precisely this: God is 'separate'. Different, very different; and to forget that would be to step over a dangerous boundary.

God warns in the book of the prophet Ezekiel:

> 'Her priests do violence to my law and profane my holy things; they do not distinguish between the holy and the common; they teach that there is no difference between the unclean and the clean; and they shut their eyes to the keeping of my Sabbaths, so that I am profaned among them.'
> EZEKIEL 22:26

In what sense is God separate and completely different? Well, if there is a God, he is not part of creation. He is, then, neither matter nor wave. Neither energy nor radiation. Because all of this only came into being when he created the universe. If God exists, he is not limited by space and time, for both began with the very beginning of creation. If there is God, then there is nothing that has caused him to be. Nothing that defines him, nothing that limits him. No concept that determines him and no category that contains him. Again, in what ways is God separate and different? To be precise, every way. 'God is holy' means he is complete, and completely different from anything we know. But this already uncomfortable statement needs to be continued, even more uncomfortably: he is complete, and completely different from anything that humans can ever come to fully recognize.

That there are insights and truths to which we still have no access, that in itself will probably not surprise anyone. Belief in the unlimited possibilities of research is firm in our time. If you allow enough time, we can solve every last riddle. Well, even if that were the case, we would still need to add one last riddle, that of Creation. Which would still be the limited knowledge of limited beings, and only of that part of reality that is based on sensory data and experience. But the truth of God's holiness is that there is something that can never – not under any circumstances – become the object of the intellectual knowledge of man. There is something against which all our senses and all our theories hopelessly fail. And it is precisely this, as the central mystery of the universe, all being and our very life. 'Si enim comprehendis, non est deus,' says Anselm the Great: 'If you understood him, he would not be God anymore.'

With that, God stands – and is finally exalted – above all that he has created. Thereto, the famous reformed theologian Karl Barth in his *Church Dogmatics* writes:

> *In comparison to everything else, God is unique – as He is and what He is – while everything else is what it is by Him, and therefore only dependently, in a contingent and figurative sense, and therefore not in a way that competes with God.*[48]

What emerges from this is, at first, a seemingly unpredictable gap between God on the one hand and his creatures on the other.

> *[God] is as high above an archangel as above a caterpillar, for the gulf that separates the archangel from the caterpillar is but finite, while the gulf between God and the archangel is infinite.*[49]

If God's being stands on its own, then, according to Thomas Aquinas, he is neither the composition of parts (for the parts must already have been before the composition, for God is not

48 Karl Barth, *Church Dogmatics II.1: The Doctrine of God* translated by T. H. L. Parker et al. (T & T Clark, 1957), p.443.
49 Aiden Wilson Tozer, *The Attributes of God.*

the result of a process), nor anything pervasive or unfamiliar.[50] It follows that God is a single unit; we creatures are complex, consisting of parts that somehow relate to each other, have tensions and fractures. God, on the other hand, is profound and complete in himself. '*I AM WHO I AM.*' (Exodus 3:14) That's what God calls himself. And Aquinas concludes: 'every name is destined to designate the nature or essence of a thing. As a result, God's being is his nature or his essence'.[51] Everything has its being in God. Therefore, in God is all perfection, so Aquinas continues in a classical ontological conclusion. For everything, a virtue exists only on the basis of its being. The wine is only good because it is actually good. The claimed speed of a car is of little use, as it only has the advantage of speed when it is going fast.

While with us – created beings – there will always be a gap between what we would like to be, what we think we are and what we could be, in God there is fullness of being. And with the fullness of being, also the fullness of every positive trait. No matter what trait distinguishes anyone whom he created, God has that quality and in perfection! 'So he can therefore not give preferences, for that could amount to something.'[52]

That God is God, and that God is infinitely exalted above all that is, is the fundamental experience of all that encounter him in biblical narratives. And so the reaction of the created to the Creator is not just an interested consideration, but is totally overpowering. Even before God says anything to anyone, his glory, his splendour, is seen. The people of Israel at Mount Sinai, Moses and the bush, Isaiah or Ezekiel in the prophetic visions of God's throne: light shines around them, its brilliance shakes them. 'Woe to me ... I am ruined!' exclaims Isaiah at the sound of the voices of the seraphim (Isaiah 6:5). God is completely different and infinitely more powerful than we weak creatures. 'A man cannot see God and stay alive': this runs like a red thread throughout the narratives of Israel. (Exodus 19:21, 33:20;

---

50 *Summa contra Gentiles I 18.*
51 *Summa contra Gentiles I 22.*
52 *Summa contra Gentiles I 28.*

Leviticus 16:2; Numbers 4:20; Judges 6:22; 13:22; Isaiah 6:5). And no one may ascertain that God is very different in the New Testament.

> For the God of the New Testament is not less holy than the God of the Old Testament, but more holy. The interval between the creature and Him is not diminished but made absolute; the unworthiness of the profane in contrast to Him is not extenuated but enhanced. That God none the less admits access to Himself and intimacy with Himself is not a mere matter of course: it is a grace beyond our power to apprehend, a prodigious paradox. To take this paradox out of Christianity is to make it shallow and superficial beyond recognition.[53]

An encounter with God in the Bible is never a harmonious sense of the depth of one's own soul, but the imposing authority of one who comes to the world, both judging and blessing.[54]

> 'To whom will you compare me?
>   Or who is my equal?' says the Holy One.
> Lift up your eyes and look to the heavens:
>   who created all these?
> He who brings out the starry host one by one
>   and calls forth each of them by name.
> Because of his great power and mighty strength,
>   not one of them is missing.
> ISAIAH 40:25–26

Such a holy God is a provocation, an unreasonable demand on his created ones, for next to him is no second. He does not even have an opponent. He is the only God. There remains only the choice to recognize him as God, to worship him or to rise against him in the delusion of rebellion. Therefore, the word of God's holiness is also a judgmental one. And so, one reads

53 Rudolf Otto, *The Idea of the Holy* (Oxford University Press 1929), p. 59.
54 Balthasar III/2 Bd 1,16.

directly before the Isaiah verses quoted above:

> *He brings princes to naught*
> *and reduces the rulers of this world to nothing.*
> *No sooner are they planted,*
> *no sooner are they sown,*
> *no sooner do they take root in the ground,*
> *than he blows on them and they wither,*
> *and a whirlwind sweeps them away like chaff.*
> ISAIAH 40:23–24

The real implications of the holiness of God and its uniqueness for the state of man in the world are evident when one reads the eloquent sentences of Karl Barth. As German tanks roll through France and Poland and the masses pay homage to a dictator by crying out '*Heil!*' to he who has made himself a judge of life and death, Barth wrote in his *Church Dogmatics*:

> *It was on the truth of the sentence that God is One that the 'Third Reich' of Adolf Hitler made shipwreck. Let this sentence be uttered in such a way that it will be heard and grasped, and at once 450 prophets of Baal are always in fear of their lives. There is no more room now for what the recent past called toleration. Beside God there are only His creatures or false gods, and beside faith in Him there are religions only as religions of superstition, error and finally irreligion.*[55]

55 Barth, *Church Dogmatics II.1*, p.444.

GOD IS NOT RELATIVE, BUT ETERNAL

God is called holy in the Bible. This characteristic is not written in abstract, but proves to be so in relation to his people. In a statement, Blaise Pascal rightly points out that God is not the God of the philosophers but of Abraham, Isaac and Jacob. The God, rather, who reveals himself to real people. And whose self-revelation, therefore, also becomes accessible to others; he also opens up to the word and to the mind of man. Abraham and his descendants experience God as the faithful God of the covenant. He is the one they can depend on and build upon. The statements about God's eternity are therefore not so much metaphysical in nature, but rather they mean: one can rely on him in every situation, he remains faithful to his promises. It is said:

> *Why do you complain, Jacob?*
>   *Why do you say, Israel,*
> *'My way is hidden from the LORD;*
>   *my cause is disregarded by my God'?*
> *Do you not know?*
>   *Have you not heard?*
> *The LORD is the everlasting God,*
>   *the Creator of the ends of the earth.*
> *He will not grow tired or weary,*
>   *and his understanding no one can fathom.*
> *He gives strength to the weary*
>   *and increases the power of the weak.*
> ISAIAH 40:27–29

God is not faithful just because he has decided to stand by his word, but because in him there is no changing (James 1:17). His being and his nature are not subject to the passage of time. That God is eternal means ultimately more than that he does not die. In fact, an endless sequence of time would not be an eternity. For time only emerged with the first creative word of God. God's relationship to time is completely different from that of us earthly beings.

'I do not have time,' we say, and by that we mean we cannot do something because we have to do something else. Because time is running out, I have something special to do. If the postbox is emptied at eleven o'clock, I have to post the letter before then, so that it can arrive on time. The dimension of time subjects me to its dictates. The yoghurt in the refrigerator has an expiry date, a day has only a certain number of hours of sunshine and the tasks of each job have a time frame in which they need to occur – of which this book is an example. The ultimate frame and the ultimate limit is death. Our life itself is 'his until death' through our being cast into space and time, so echo the philosophers.

'I have time' in this context is therefore a deceptive metaphor, because what do we 'have' if we have 'time'? Do we not rather mean: the basic situation of man is that time has us under its control? And that you can be grateful if there are a few hours or days or even weeks when its grip is less noticeable, because there is less to do? Although the grip itself is not loosened, we do not actually have more time, but during that same time, fewer things to do.

Our limitation by time is a situation of subjugation. We cannot go back in time and we cannot go into the future. Even though I was once in the past and I will also be in the future! But my life, my being, is given to me only in defined portions that are now administered. My life has either passed away or is still ahead of me: obviously, I only 'have' this moment. Apparently tangible and if I really want to grab it, it's already over. Childhood ends when it becomes youth. Youth ends when it comes to adulthood. Whether sprouting, growing, flowering, ripening, fruiting and dying: all this is in the nature of being, just not at the same time. One stage must always cease or end when the next one comes. Life in time is a state of existence that is constantly being denied something. The freedom of our being is profoundly constrained, since the inexorable limit of time highlights the barrier to our limited human existence. 'All joy wants eternity – Wants deep, wants deep eternity.'[56] Nietzsche lets his Zarathustra sing, but it

56 Nietzsche, *Also sprach Zarathustra*, IV, 12, p. 264.

is in vain. So beyond this limit what would a human being be? They would be a deeply free being.

If God is not part of his creation, but rather its author, then he is not subject to its laws. In fact, fundamentally God is subject to neither standard, nor rule, nor category and under no obligation outside of himself. God is free. And because he is free, he is also free from the decay of time. In his book *The Consolation of Philosophy* (Volume 6), the late Roman Christian philosopher Boethius states: '*Aeternitas est interminabilis vitae tota simul et perfecta possessio*'; that is: 'Eternity is at one and the same time the complete and perfect possession of unlimited life'.[57] That which we earthly creatures do not know is in God. 'At every beginning magic dwells within', says Hermann Hesse, just to explain that the magic remains far too brief. In God, the beginning, the prevailing and the completion, can be together. 'Eternity is just the duration which is lacking to time.'[58]

However, that God is eternal does not mean that he cannot have contact with his created beings within time. Neither does it mean that he is just static: in him is vibrant life, dynamism and action. He is not, however, subject to all this. Time does not 'have' him. He alone really has time. '*Totum esse suum simul habens*', says Aquinas: 'He has his own being, all at the same time'.[59]

What does this mean for the person who believes in and lives with God? Who lives in a time that is constantly changing and basically assumes that progress is always a move in the right direction? Is this faith in an eternal God a strong anchor? It was exactly this anchor when God introduced himself to the patriarchs: 'Abraham planted a tamarisk tree in Beersheba, and there he called on the name of the LORD, the Eternal God.' (Genesis 21:33) The God-fearing man knows that God never comes too late. That he does not grow old and does not think about abdicating. That his intentions and his schedules are

---

57 Our translation.
58 Barth, *Church Dogmatics II.1, p.608*.
59 Summa contra Gentiles I 15.

perfect. A thousand years are nothing to God. God is never in a hurry, and this saying is true: 'God's mills grind slowly but exceedingly fine'.

The belief in such a God who does not care about the latest trend. Whether a particular truth is called contemporary, up to date, progressive, or rather old-fashioned, reactionary and conservative, will appear to be relatively uninteresting from the perspective of eternity. If God is eternal, then he is neither the God of the past nor the present nor the future. And the message from him will never be contemporary and it never was, if rightly proclaimed! The word of God is not relative, such that it changes for each generation. All our times and epochs are relative to the eternity of God. But also our traditions, our favourite rituals and cultural customs are, and remain, time-dependent: God alone is the Eternal. Salvation is not in the past; anyone who has realized that will live differently. 'Those who do not have time are those who do not have eternity either,'[60] Barth writes – is he not right?

When God is eternal, what happened when he took on human form in Jesus Christ becomes even more fully evident. When God becomes our contemporary, descending into the confines of space and time, he acts in it at the same time as God. Jesus is true man and true God. But if God speaks and acts as God, these are words and actions that are not confined to the Roman provinces of Judea and Galilee around AD 30. All attempts to understand Jesus only from his era fail, not only for historical but also for theological reasons. Of course, Jesus was also a child of his time. But as God he is not subject to the limitations of time. He became human and submits to them voluntarily. But by doing so: 'He masters time. He re-creates it and heals its wounds, the fleetingness of the present, and the separation of past and the future from one another and from the present'.[61] What Jesus did then is present today and real, because he 'is the same yesterday and today and forever' (Hebrews 13:8).

60 Barth, *Church Dogmatics II.1*, p.612.
61 Barth, *Church Dogmatics II.1*, p.617.

But we do not have to do a contextualisation into today's language, or be culturally relevant or otherwise be up to date. Rather, it's about us coming into his time. He does not offer to come into our world, but offers believers access into his: 'Now this is eternal life: that they know you, the only true God, and Jesus Christ, whom you have sent,' says Jesus (John 17:3), and speaks of *aeonic* life – that is, not just life in the infinite long term, but in God's infinite reality. What a completely new world view! In Jesus Christ, the eternal God – historically unique – comes to his creation and offers, to the one who believes in him, a completely changed state of life. 'Real created time acquires in Jesus Christ and in every act of faith in Him the character and stamp of eternity, and life in it acquires the special characteristics of eternal life.'[62] For in Jesus Christ we become God's contemporaries.

The Power of Now is the name of the bestseller by Eckhart Tolle, usually found in a corner of the bookshop on the esoteric shelves, where the self-help and counselling books are found. The realization that dwelling in the past or a constant concern for the future is a paralyzing force, and that the present moment is the only genuinely creative space, does not stem from either time and motion studies or westernized forms of Buddhism. It stands for what Christians might call fulfilled time. The true being, into which eternity enters, in whose overflowing well and inexhaustible ocean is the eternal God.

GOD IS NOT HELPLESS, BUT ALMIGHTY

The oldest creed of Christianity starts, right at the beginning, with this: '*Credo in Deum Patrem omnipotentem*'. Or, translated: 'I believe in God the Father Almighty'. So God is a Father and he is almighty. Both aspects were contested from the very beginning of the Christian Church. His fatherhood means that

---

62 Barth, *Church Dogmatics II.1*, p.617.

Jesus Christ is his true Son and his omnipotence means that he has no rival. Contrary to Christian heresies, which deny the fatherhood of God, Christ is known as the true Son. Contrary to the teachings of the Manichaeans (and some common beliefs about the devil that still exist today), the church emphasizes from the beginning that there is no evil anti-god but just the one and only God, and that he is omnipotent. Even evil is no competition for God; the devil is nothing more than a fallen but created archangel. God is in full possession of all power and even the evil of the world does not step out of the narrowly defined playing field that God has himself set.

All these statements follow seamlessly from the previous section. Everything that God is, he is through himself. This also means that he is not governed by any external law. He is not righteous because he lives a righteous life. Righteousness is – that is, there is such a thing as righteousness – only because God was first righteous. God is also not good because he fulfils the criterion of 'good', or because he behaves in accordance with goodness, rather goodness only exists because God is good. That which is righteous, good and true, is first determined by God's being.

Now what is the name of a being that is not limited to anything external in his actions? It is called almighty. If God is almighty, then he can do what he wants. And that is exactly the biblical message:

> Our God is in heaven;
>> he does whatever pleases him.
>
> PSALMS 115:3

He is the sovereign, happy ruler of the universe. Impressively, the Bible proves this – his unqualified authority. To King Cyrus, the conqueror of whole kingdoms, God speaks in the book of the prophet Isaiah:

> 'I am the LORD, and there is no other;
>> apart from me there is no God.

I will strengthen you,
     though you have not acknowledged me,
so that from the rising of the sun
     to the place of its setting
people may know there is none besides me.
     I am the LORD, and there is no other.
I form the light and create darkness,
     I bring prosperity and create disaster;
     I, the LORD, do all these things.'

ISAIAH 45:5–7

The testimony of the sovereignty of God runs across all strata of the biblical tradition: God creates and chooses, God calls and punishes, God saves and rejects. Behind all human history, God remains the one who is actually active. He is the one who employs rulers and it is he who directs even the hearts of kings like streams of water (Proverbs 21:1), who determines the times and the ages for whole nations, as he pleases. At the same time, he is the God who counts every hair on your head (Luke 12:7), and not a sparrow falls to earth without our Father knowing (Matthew 10:29).

Behind every event and behind every decision is God! Where then is humanity and our freedom, we might ask? And this touches on one of the great questions in the history of theology. If God is omnipotent, can people have free will? How do human freedom and God's omnipotence relate to each other?

All answers to this question oscillate between two extremes. And both extremes are theologically unacceptable. On the one hand, a God who does what he wants. Consequently, people are without a will, automatons at the mercy of a divine arbitrariness. People are as puppets or as spectators in a cosmic theatre which runs according to a script that has long been defined to the last detail.

The biblical testimony contradicts this interpretation in many places. Humanity is repeatedly confronted with the decision that was first posed in the garden by God. They are responsible for their actions and cannot claim to be unable to do otherwise, because they do not have free will. In fact, people are voting against what God really wants. God responds and demands a decision, a decision that people have to make themselves. People are called to believe, to obey, to return, to choose the good and not the evil: 'I have set before you life and death, blessings and curses. Now choose life, so that you and your children may live' (Deuteronomy 30:19). People can choose.

An extreme sovereignty of God, one which disempowers people, cannot be the right image of God's omnipotence. Just as wrong, and perhaps even more dangerous, is another extreme: a nice kind God who needs our help. A God who allows people to be so free to choose and decide that he himself is limited by us. Touching and well known is the photograph of a crucifix from a bombed church. The carved image of Christ has lost hands and legs and a well-meaning believer has attached a sign over it: 'Now all I have left is your hands and legs'. What is meant is that it is through our deeds of love that the love of God is made visible to the eyes of the people.

This picture, already used a thousand times in group lessons, church services and in religious books, is as appealing as it is fundamentally wrong. Of course, the world should recognize the love of God in the disciples of Jesus (John 13:35), and of course it is a mission and calling of every Christian, through his or her life, to give a vivid testimony to the goodness of God. It is also true that courageous action, actively caring for our neighbour, is required – not just pious navel gazing, trusting that God will do everything himself. God is not and has never been limited to the abilities of the people who serve him. If God cooperates with people in his plan, it is never because he needs their help. It is far more the case that God complains, again and again, that we do not trust him enough:

> *Surely the arm of the LORD is not too short to save,*
> *nor his ear too dull to hear.*
> ISAIAH 59:1

Why, then, involve people at all? Why social commitment, preaching or even prayer, when God can do everything alone anyway? Because God is community and wants fellowship, he acts together with people. He would like to involve them voluntarily in his work of salvation and calls us to this. He does this because he wants to share his perspective. Because he wants to teach people how to love. And because he wants to glorify himself by using weak and fragile human vessels for his grand plan, which surpasses the capacity of these very people, so much so that in the end he will be praised. And so Paul can in the same breath name both his own efforts, and God's work in them. 'To this end I strenuously contend with all the energy Christ so powerfully works in me.' (Colossians 1:29)

While both extremes always lead to theological distortion, it should first be noted that a clear accentuation of God's omnipotence does not in any way lead to the passivity of humankind. This is especially evident in intercessory prayer. 'What else is revealed when God hears and answers prayer but that He is the Creator and Lord of all things?'[63] He is thus completely free and sovereign Lord of all. But out of love, he looks and he longs for people to cooperate with him by choice. But even this free decision of man is not made on neutral ground. 'You did not choose me, but I chose you,' Jesus tells his disciples (John 15:16a); and remember that God is over both the temporal and the eternal. Before anyone can say 'Yes' to him, this is preceded by a divine 'Yes'. And in such a mysterious way that God's election always remains pure grace. God is completely free and completely omnipotent. If we believe in him, we add nothing to his happiness. He alone is God.

He is God and omnipotent, even where evil is happening. God does not actively will, want or wish for, the presence of evil; however, his plan and his rule are not tarnished by it. Rather, in spite of the occurrence of evil and despite the rebellion of sin, his plans will be fulfilled. This leads us back to the previously

---

63 Barth, *Church Dogmatics II.1*, p.512.

raised theodicy problem with a new focus: does God want evil to happen, or does he not want it? Barth tries to solve the apparent dilemma:

> [God] wills [evil] in so far as He gives it this space, position and function. He does not do so as its author, recognising it as His creature, approving and confirming and vindicating it. On the contrary, He wills it as He denies it His authorship, as He refuses it any standing before Him or right or blessing or promise, as He places it under His prohibition and curse and treats it as that from which He wishes to redeem and liberate His creation. In this way, then, in His turning away from it, He wills what He disavows. It cannot exist without Him. It, too, is by Him, and is under His control and government. There is nothing that is withdrawn from His will, just as there is nothing hidden from His knowledge. There is no sphere of being or non-being which is not in some way wholly subject to His will … His will is therefore done in all and by all.[64]

It is when contemplating the secrets of the divine omnipotence that Paul, at the end of his discussion about the role of Israel and the Gentiles, exclaims:

> Oh, the depth of the riches of the wisdom and knowledge of God!
>> How unsearchable his judgments,
>> and his paths beyond tracing out!
> 'Who has known the mind of the Lord?
>> Or who has been his counsellor?'
> 'Who has ever given to God,
>> that God should repay them?'
> ROMANS 11:33–35

---

64 Barth, *Church Dogmatics II.1*, p.565 ff.

Here is the end of all human questioning and the beginning of all wisdom: God is almighty and knows exactly what he is doing. Whether we can understand his intentions or not does not change anything, his will will be done.

•˙•˳•˙•˳•˙● ●˳•˙•˳•˙•˳

TEARS IN RIGA

Outside, a tram rumbles past and night falls over the weathered glitter of the Latvian capital. Red brick and Soviet concrete. In the middle of Riga, I kneel on the floor of a simple hotel. Splendid art nouveau facade and creaking staircases, but shabby bathrooms. I also feel a bit like that inside. How could it turn out like this? It had started so well. All the plans my team and I had been working on for months were now shattered. That God is sovereign and able to do what he wants is theoretically familiar to me. But experiencing it so close up is a little less enjoyable. And so tears well up in my eyes that evening in Riga.

For six years now our House of Prayer project has been in existence. We started out with much idealism and great dedication. The dream of a handful of young adults has become a dynamic initiative with annual conferences, training and many visitors. At the centre of everything: the prayer room, which will be discussed again in the next chapter. Over time, the place in the small electrical shop which we had rented had become too restricted and it was not exactly what might be called comfortable, as in the winter it was so cold that the windows froze thick inside, and in the summer it was as hot as a greenhouse. Then, in prayer, came the clear impression that we should look for a property. We quickly found the ideal place. Only the conversion costs were estimated at 400,000 euros, an astronomical amount for us. Once again, in prayer, came the sudden idea to seek supporters who would each be willing to give 1,000 euros, and to find exactly 400 of them.

With much faith we started and called the project 'David's Oath' as, after all, King David had put aside money for the construction of the sanctuary. Shortly after launching the project, I got in touch with an experienced finance manager who agreed to coordinate the fundraising. With over-zealous enthusiasm, flyers were printed, presentations made and letters sent. And indeed, more and more donations were coming in. Negotiations with the owner of the property went well at first, but then became increasingly difficult. Finally, we were forced to break off negotiations shortly before our big conference, where we had wanted to advertise our New House of Prayer Centre. Here we stood, without a building. Countless conversations and a complete architectural plan for the property all suddenly seemed to have been in vain. God, why?

But the donations were now mounting up so that our attention quickly turned to another property that was for sale. A few months ago we had not so much as entertained the idea of such a building, because the price seemed unattainable. But we could not lose this opportunity; we immediately entered into negotiations regarding the purchase. It was indicated to us that we would get the building, so we started fundraising with all our might for the final push. At the conference, we proudly presented our new plans. Advertising, attending to the donors, information on the Internet and countless meetings for 'David's Oath' – our well-oiled machine was running smoothly. The grand finale was to be a solemn support meeting with gala dinner, where you could visit the new house and make a donation towards it.

Seven days before the deadline, I call the seller to confirm the inspection appointment. I cannot believe what I hear on the phone. Apparently, we had not contacted him for a few weeks, he was no longer convinced of our intention to purchase and meanwhile, another buyer had outbid us, and their purchase of the building had been legally agreed. This knocks the wind out of me. The only possibility, the voice on the phone says, is that the situation could still change, in that the bank may not agree to accept the funding for the purchase. This will be decided by Friday. If you have not heard from me by Friday, you should assume that the building has been sold.

It's that same Friday that I fly to Riga to speak at a conference. The evening before, we hold a meeting with our leadership team. We sit drinking tea and wondering what all this means. Through perplexity and inner dismay Petra says the crucial words: 'This cannot be a coincidence. God is wanting to tell us something.' But what is he wanting to say? Was it not his will that we build a house of prayer? Was it not all about him? Or maybe not? Others from the team joined in: 'We got so carried away'. And I felt what was really the case, acutely: 'Johannes you have lost your way', because I had jumped in pretty much alone, together with Josef, our finance manager. It had gone so well that, at some point, I really did not know anymore whether it was all about my own plans or God's honour. A realization that weighed heavily on me, and pushed me to the ground.

Munich Airport, Gate H 84. One last look at my mobile phone: of course nobody has called and now it is Friday afternoon. The fleeting thought of making another call, setting all levers in motion. I decide against it. The message is already so obvious. Despite all attempts, despite all the planning and despite all the money, my dreams have been smashed for the second time in a row and lie in pieces at my feet. I felt clearly: obviously, God did not want this project to happen that way. His ways work differently. But how should I explain it to all our supporters? That they have donated for something that now doesn't exist? The meeting is only five days away. I am already ashamed now. I spend all weekend in Riga in an inner state of repentance. Not repenting as an act of self-flagellation, but as the bitter realization that I have confused God's plans with my own. And now, capitulation. In the dust before God's sovereignty. This is something I had not reckoned with. I myself had planned and done it all. And due to this, God's guidance had been lost, but only now do I realize this. Days of deep humiliation and uncertainty in Riga. I had tried everything and thereby had lost my way. If anything should happen now, it would be a sovereign act of God. On Friday the conversation with the bank should have taken place, but even Monday passes without a word. It is one thing to talk about God's omnipotence, but another to acknowledge it in one's life.

It is already evening, when suddenly my telephone rings. If we are willing to sign immediately, we can buy the building. The other buyer's plans have spontaneously fallen through. Tears of gratitude. Four days later, the purchase contract is signed and our donors can visit the house. And how does it look financially? We have exactly the right amount in our account to pay for the building without going into debt. There are exactly 400 David's Oath godparents. Not 398 and not 403, but exactly 400. And ever since, there has been a House of Prayer Centre in Augsburg.

Since those tearful days in Riga, it has never crossed my mind to think of this project as something that has been done and planned by people. To this day there remains a sense of holy awe. The salutary fright before God's sovereignty. It is we who want to build up his kingdom who must realize that he always remains the agent, and he reminds us of this fact when we start to drift into forgetfulness. And to his friends he also remains Lord, the Father, the Almighty.

GOD IS NOT YOUR MATE, BUT JUDGE

The wrath of the gods. Whether it is Poseidon with his trident as the explanation for a storm at sea, or the Germanic Thor's hammer as cause of a thunderstorm, folk tales and mythology are full of the idea of gods who are angry, who like to punish and take revenge.

Such ideas are alien to us today, because we know the physical causes behind our weather systems. And to imagine an angry God might also seem questionable for theological reasons. What is there for him to be angry about, if he is omnipotent?

But God is not only depicted in the Bible as omnipotent or transcendental, but also, amazingly, in an emotional way. God rejoices over his people (Zephaniah 3:17) and mourns over their faithlessness. Yes, in his sadness he almost sounds like a disappointed lover:

> *'Does a young woman forget her jewellery,*
> *a bride her wedding ornaments?*
> *Yet my people have forgotten me,*
> *days without number.'*
> JEREMIAH 2:32

God is moved by compassion and mercy; his feelings are portrayed as strong, unconstrained power:

> *'My heart is changed within me;*
> *all my compassion is aroused.'*
> HOSEA 11:8C

And God loves. And not just in a general or ethereal way, but he loves like a bridegroom. These are amazing images, in which again and again the relationship of Israel to God is depicted as a love bond between a wife and her husband:

> *'Go and proclaim in the hearing of Jerusalem:*
> *This is what the LORD says:*
> *"I remember the devotion of your youth,*
> *how as a bride you loved me*
> *and followed me through the wilderness,*
> *through a land not sown."'*
> JEREMIAH 2:2

And finally,

> *As a young man marries a young woman,*
>   *so will your Builder marry you;*
> *as a bridegroom rejoices over his bride,*
>   *so will your God rejoice over you.*
> ISAIAH 62:5

God's love is not a universal love for everything and everyone, but it is a federal love, an exclusive love. God longs for reciprocated love. And that is why the words that the prophets speak are, at the same time, words of love as well as admonition; in Jeremiah's case his heart is even burning. (Jeremiah 5:14).

> *But the word burns only because in God himself his jealousy burns: suddenly, as never before, we are given a glimpse into the heart of God: this jealousy, therefore, says so much about his spiritual being, because it is jealousy's unique choice, and refers to the uniqueness of those living as, free, sovereign subjects and reveals the point where their choice can become either a consuming love or the all-consuming punishing blaze.*[65]

God's love is as a burning love. And in that love, he can be jealous and therefore angry.

God's wrath is a recurring biblical theme. To downplay it for reasons of consideration for today's values is to alienate the Christian image of God. God is angry. He is not angry even though he is love and even though he is holy, but for this very reason. This provocative statement loses its offensiveness if we consider that there is more or less legitimate anger and more or less righteous anger. So the anger of a motorist who receives a speeding ticket is perhaps understandable, but hardly justified. On the other hand, there is also righteous anger. Anger that calls injustice by name and allows itself to be moved emotionally. It is such anger that

---

65 Balthasar, *Herrlichkeit III,2.1.*

makes Orsina exclaim in Gotthold Ephraim Lessing's bourgeois tragedy *Emilia Galotti*: 'They who, under certain circumstances do not lose their intellect, have none to lose.'[66]

God is angry because he hates that which is wrong. The idea of a god who is left cold, unmoved by murder, expulsion, rape and exploitation is horrific. He hates that which is opposed to love. What kind of love would that be if a father were to be emotionally indifferent to the criminal attempting to kidnap his child? Love for the child will cause the father to fight anything that harms his child. A loving father will hate the drugs that destroy a teenager's life. He will not feel indifference towards them.

The question of whether God can be angry about sin is ultimately the question of whether God is a judge and whether hell exists. These are questions that embarrass enlightened Christians of the twenty-first century and which they would prefer to ignore, like the irritating peculiarities of a visiting old aunt, which one would prefer not to expose in public. But the Bible teaches that God's wrath and his judicial work are part of his nature. And while God is always the same, the human heart can turn in different directions, even in directions diametrically opposed to love and truth. To oppose the nature of God.

Perhaps the most widespread theological error of modern times is that of universal reconciliation, which maintains that all go to heaven. 'For him whose striving never ceases we can provide redemption,'[67] says the angel in *Faust II*, the convenient customer. This theory is fed either by trivializing human guilt or trivializing God. If sin is seen as something which man really cannot do anything about, and which could be avoided by a little empathy and better conditions, then hell or even the judgment of God is simply superfluous. But both the Bible and human history bear such a grim graphic testimony to the existence of evil in man, that one would have to take leave of reality in order to dismiss sin as a peripheral issue.

---

66 *The Dramatic Works of G E Lessing* edited by Ernest Bell *Emilia Galotti* Act IV, 7 (George Bell and Sons, 1878).
67 Goethe, *Faust II*, V, *Bergschluchten* (11935).

'*Nondum considerasti quanti ponderis sit peccatum*', answers Anselm in his treatise *Cur deus homo (Why God became Man)* on the suggestion of his interlocutor that God can forgive sin 'just like that': 'You have not yet considered how heavy the weight of sin is.'[68]

In the light of God everything becomes visible, nothing can be hidden:

> *Nothing in all creation is hidden from God's sight. Everything is uncovered and laid bare before the eyes of him to whom we must give account.*
> HEBREWS 4:13

Because God is holy and because God is truth, an insurmountable chasm lies between us and God. The teaching of God's judgment is not that there are good and less good people and that those with the most good deeds eventually go to heaven. The doctrine of the judgment of God states that this world is under the judgment of God. Jesus came into a world that lies under the power of evil. And so, the proclamation of the early church is not, 'Be good people, so that you may be rewarded'. But, 'Save yourselves from this corrupt generation.' (Acts 2:40b) And finally, in the first chapter of the Epistle to the Romans – at the beginning of the gospel discourse, mind:

> *The wrath of God is being revealed from heaven against all the godlessness and wickedness of people, who suppress the truth by their wickedness.*
> ROMANS 1:18

That God is a judge does not mean that he imposes a penalty on people from outside that has nothing to do with them. His judgments spring from his truthfulness: it reveals with horrible consistency the real consequences of the decisions that

---

68 'Why God Became Man' in *Anselm of Canterbury The Major Works* edited by Brian Davies and G R Evans (Oxford University Press, 1998), p.305.

mankind has made. But every sin always carries a punishment within itself. For the one who is proud, for the one who is egotistical, payment for their arrogance is loneliness. For the one who is aggressive and violent, for them the relationships that are most important to them will be destroyed.

However, the punishment that every sin carries within itself can remain invisible for a long time. The alcoholic will only gradually, and perhaps far too late and probably never, be made fully aware of the consequences of a life of alcoholism. 'A man reaps what he sows' (Galatians 6:7b). And while good habits in humans do not usually develop of their own accord, the egotistical and petty traits of a person usually increase over the course of their life. It seems to be the essence of evil to proliferate. And so they are also metaphors of growth that are found in the Bible when it comes to hell: it's about a burning fire, devouring worms (Mark 9:48). It may be a small flame that sets fire to a house: but it is eventually consumed by it. That is exactly the essence of evil. You might decide to play a little, and soon without realizing it, it is no longer you who is playing the game, but the game itself plays you.

Sin grows. And because man has received an immortal soul from God, the consequences of sin do not end with death: they are eternal. When the house burns, it cannot extinguish itself.

Sin grows by itself and it is the opposite of God's essence. Besides all the interpersonal, health and emotional harm caused by this deceiver, the most serious is the separation from God. That the creature which owes all it has to the Creator cuts itself off from the only source of life, joy and love – this is truly the greatest drama of the universe. It is the worst that can happen. So awful that Jesus asks his disciples not to fear even violent death by comparison (Matthew 10:28).

Some Christians claim that only the God of the Old Testament speaks of judgment and punishment. But it is precisely our 'gentle' Jesus who says more about hell than any other biblical figure, and warns against it.[69] Not because his message is not good news in the end, and he just wants to scare people. He warns out of love. Anyone who energetically yanks his child off the tracks might seem brutal at first glance. But if you see the rapidly approaching freight train, you understand that they need to take a hastier approach. And so Jesus does not, nor do the New Testament writers, tire of warning us of the real danger of being eternally lost. (A small selection of instances: Matthew 8:12; 10:28; 13:42, 50; 18:6–9; 22:13; 23:33; 24:51; 25:30, 41; Mark 9:43–48; Luke 13:28; 2 Thessalonians 1:6–9; Jude 7; Revelation 14:9–11; 20:10, 14.)

This is exactly the message of the 'lostness' of mankind – that is all people – which forms the foundation of the gospel. This basis is lacking when one reduces the story of Jesus to the example of a good-hearted social worker. Lost is the message that no one can save himself by his own power. For who would be powerful enough to heal the distortion of the human heart from within? Who would be able to give someone a 'new heart'? (Ezekiel 36:26) It would have to be a god. But with that, the reconciliation between God and mankind would not have been accomplished; for this to happen always requires a mutual approach from both sides. But who would be capable of assuming responsibility for the unfathomable abyss or morass of human sin, so that they could ask for forgiveness and redress? Human sin is not just an emotional mood: it is a real problem that screams for a real remedy. Our sense of injustice bears witness to this. The damage is not resolved by someone saying they are sorry. There would only be a reconciliation between God and humanity if a person takes the place of the sinner, someone who then takes responsibility for it. But a person who would have to bear the result and consequences of all these sins. Namely the entire burden of the entire debt. The loneliness, the shame, the anguish and finally the total separation from God.

It would be a person who would need to die a thousand deaths. That's exactly what the gospel message is. That there

69 One of the most helpful and illuminating books for understanding the disturbing theme of eternal loss is not theological, but narrative: C. S. Lewis, *The Great Divorce* (Collins, 2012).

actually is *such a one!* A mediator between God and man. One who is able to become the representative of all sinful people. He is human. And one who is at the same time able to bear all the consequences of sin. One who loved enough to give his life for it. One who loved completely and exclusively and always. Who accepted the place in the dock and received the court verdict that had been given to us. The condemnation to death. Who experienced the separation from God in his own body and mind. He offered us his place: the place of one before God, the place of the Father's Son. A mediator, after all, who was not only able to offer this way, but also to fulfil it in reality. He who did not remain in death but overcame even the last and final consequence of sin – death. Who rose from the grave and opened a way for anyone who believes in him. A path to reconciliation with God, the definitive end of the separation between man and God that came through sin.

Yes, God is a judge. But he is at the same time the one who stands on the side of the accused:

> *Very truly I tell you, whoever hears my word and believes him who sent me has eternal life and will not be judged but has crossed over from death to life.'*
> JOHN 5:24

• • • • • • • • • • • ● ●• • • • • • • • • •

HOPE FOR ELDERLY ELISABETH

Bent almost double, she hauls herself into the kitchen to make tea. There is a smell of garlic and lard; pink artificial flowers and a picture of Jesus on the beige plastic tablecloth. She has to laugh about her clumsy hands, swollen by rheumatism so that she can no longer hold the small teaspoon. It is always in moments like this that get her started. They had to work with camels. Chop wood in the forest. Or plough the fields somewhere on the Kazakh steppe. Housed in the simplest of barracks, snow several metres high in winter. Yes, but for her things went fairly well. Her brother was shot dead at the start. Stalin did not like them, the ethnic Germans, in Russia. And so she remembers what it was like when the soldiers came to the small village with the muddy road and the wooden church. And her father had to go to Siberia. She heard nothing from him ever again. Behind someone's house they shot her brother. Bullet to the head. What is the value of a human life anyway? The women sent into forced labour. In cattle wagons, heading east and nobody knew for how many years.

I didn't meet her until she was over eighty. Her face, under the patterned headscarf, was a sea of wrinkles. What had her eyes seen? She always wore an apron, and every morning she stepped into the church, very slowly, step by step. Her generation had been stolen from her: father, brother, husband and sons. Shot dead in the war, starved to death in the Gulag, arrested in the middle of the night and gone forever. Villages burned down, girls raped, resettled and expelled. Eventually, one day, to end up stranded in the land of some distant ancestors: Germany. The country whose language she spoke with such an accent that no one knew whether she was Russian or German. A life without a home, from either side.

No home, no foothold. A woman who sought to have a firm foothold in God. The rosary always wrapped around her hand when, with a benevolent smile, she opened the door into the small flat full of carpets and kitschy murals. For hours I listened to her. Of worship services in secret. Of the visits of the secret police. Of the deaths of so many. But first and foremost: of God, of the Saviour. And in my mind is the question: who will give this old widow, for once, her rights? Who counts the tears of such women? Do such fates flow aimlessly like a trickle in the expanse of the Wadden Sea? Or are the ones who seek revenge right? Are those who want to pay back *those up there* right? Those who dream of retribution? But what retribution can there be, for such injustice?

Elisabeth's gaze was always drawn to the cross, a cross crowned with thorns. And I know that her hope is in the judge.

A judge who does not forget the millions of stories like hers. But who sees that justice is done and punishes wrong.

A LITTLE EXERCISE

At the end of this chapter are some suggestions for application. All statements about the nature of God ultimately remain head knowledge and mere theory, where they do not become a dialogue with God himself. It is not a concept that can be understood or processed. He is a person to talk to. But not an imaginary postbox for self-talk and wishes to the universe, but a person who rightly gets our attention. He is to be worshipped.

Perhaps not every reader may feel like worshipping this wild, untamed and extraordinary God, especially after the last chapter. But this is exactly where our destiny as people can be fulfilled. Of course, nobody can do that for you, but if you have become curious, here is a suggestion: pick up a Bible. Which translation you choose is not of any great importance. A good compromise between readability and textual fidelity is provided by any standard translation. You may like to try the NIV as it is both readable and as accurate a translation as any.

Now look for the book of Psalms. This book has 150 psalms, arranged as 150 chapters. You can start reading anywhere, wherever you want. Pick up a pen and a piece of paper and begin to write down the attributes of God that strike you. Sometimes you have to lift a statement from a sentence. Thus, from the verse:

> *Those who know your name trust in you,*
> *for you, LORD, have never forsaken those who seek you.*
> PSALM 9:10

The statement concludes that God is reliable and trustworthy. In your notebook or on your slip of paper you can now write:

'God you are trustworthy'. Keep going until you've found about ten such properties, whether you've been through just a few verses or longer phrases from several psalms.

In a second step you can now slowly speak these qualities back to God. Repeat individual sentences until you have the impression that the words have really reached you. It does not require your acute concentration: the divine word is truth and unfolds its power independently of our own mental abilities. Do this as long as you want, but for at least ten minutes: you should take your time, so you can also come to rest inside. You will see, this simple exercise will broaden your vocabulary in prayer and increase your ability to perceive and be amazed by God's presence. Worship, according to the experience of the worshippers, makes life deep and rich. It is the way out into an ocean of amazing wonders.

7

EXODUS

ENCOUNTER WITH BEAUTY

The question of worship is the central question of the Bible. 'The LORD, the God of the Hebrews, has sent me to say to you: let my people go, so that they may worship me in the wilderness.' (Exodus 7:16) God allows Pharaoh to be directed by Moses. Yes, God is the liberator. But liberation is more than extracting people from slavery, more than salvation from sin or from hell. It is about a liberation into a new reality, namely, 'that they may worship me'. This passage shows that the deeper meaning and purpose of God's redemptive action is for people to be free to worship God. Earlier, in Chapter 3, the basic biblical pattern was traced – the pattern according to which humankind was created by the glorious God, as his counterpart who perceives his glory and answers it with praise. This is the fulfilment of God's plan, and in it the destiny of humankind is fulfilled: that in all things God is glorified by humanity, who receive a share in his joy and his light. We humans are created for worship! The only beings who are receptive to this otherwise purposeless beauty. We alone can marvel at a painting, listen attentively to a symphony, gaze spellbound up at the cross-vaulted ceiling of a cathedral or appreciate the interwoven words of an intoxicating piece of rhyming verse. Anyone who sees something beautiful and stands amazed can't even begin to answer the question of what it does for him when he looks at it. Whether there even is a reason to be amazed. That it is beautiful is in itself the reason. The beautiful has its own evidential value. God as happy, God as glorious and God as beauty.

In an encounter with beauty, something of man's vocation – to open himself completely to that overpowering beauty and to lose oneself in worship – shines out. In his wonderful work *The Glory of the Lord*, which he characteristically calls *Theological Aesthetics*, Hans-Urs von Balthasar writes:

> *Before the beautiful – no, not really before but within the beautiful – the whole person quivers. He not only 'finds' the beautiful moving; rather, he experiences himself as being moved and possessed by it. The more total this experience is, the less does a person seek and enjoy only the delight that comes through the senses or even through any act of his own; the less also does he reflect on his own acts and states. Such a person has been taken up wholesale into the reality of the beautiful and is now fully subordinate to it, determined by it, animated by it. In so far as such experiences are sublime moments and elevations of existence and are also experienced and valued as such; in so far as the beautiful, as such, exercises its function of total integration and can be made intelligible only as a completion of the edifice comprised of the transcendental attributes of Being: to this extent it borders on the religious ...*[70]

HALLOWED

The meaning of human life is fulfilled in worship. And so it is not surprising that the prayer that Jesus teaches his disciples begins after the salutation with the words, 'Hallowed be your name!' (Matthew 6:9b) The name of God shall be hallowed,

70 Hans Urs von Balthasar, *The Glory of the Lord, A Theological Aesthetics, Vol I: Seeing the Form*, translated by Erasmo Leiva-Merikakis (T&T Clark, 1982).

held holy. But how should the name be hallowed? Of course, the praying person does not sanctify the name of God. His request that the name be hallowed expresses his decision that he will personally hold him as holy, in his life. And this decision is made in prayer, as Jesus taught, in the first place.

To hallow something means to make it the object of highest attention. If one were to say, 'That is sacred to me', that would mean: 'Nobody touches what's mine and if I have to give up everything else, under no circumstances will I give that away. Nobody touch that, because that is sacred to me, that is my treasure!'

When Jesus teaches on prayer, he puts that desire that God will be our treasure in the first part of the prayer. Why? Apparently because this is not usually the case.

Jesus' teaching on prayer comes in the context of the Sermon on the Mount. He contrasts the praying, fasting and almsgiving of the hypocrites with what his disciples should do. And how do hypocrites pray?

> And when you pray, do not be like the hypocrites, for they love to pray standing in the synagogues and on the street corners to be seen by others. Truly I tell you, they have received their reward in full.
> MATTHEW 6:5

A hypocrite is defined as a person who does something, but really they mean something else. A hypocrite pretends to be friendly, even though they are not. They are only being friendly to achieve something. A hypocrite is actually pursuing another goal. What is the goal these praying hypocrites are pursuing? They are concerned with their reputation among the people. They do not pray for the sake of prayer, but to gain something by it. Something they are really into. What is most important to them are the things they really care about. That is probably the way most people pray. One prays for a partner. Another for a job for their grown-up child. The soldier prays for a safe homecoming and others pray before an operation in hospital – becoming more than a little devout, especially in the face of death.

And this is understandable: who does not value their physical health, their personal freedom, the lives of their loved ones? Life, love, health – these are sacred to me. That which is sacred to me will determine how I pray. However, once I receive it, prayer soon falls silent. When the patient is allowed to leave hospital, they return to a prayerless daily routine. When the grown-up son finally finds a job, the mother's work is done. And when the soldier sets foot once more on his native soil, his thoughts are many and varied, but no longer directed to God and to prayer. Need teaches us to pray, but once that need is met, the lesson of prayer is quickly forgotten. That which was ultimately at stake, that which was the object of our highest yearning and our deepest concern, is either finally sanctified, or it is no longer. Therefore, at the beginning of the instruction on prayer, Jesus asks us to make God the centre of our prayer. Make him the treasure of life. The highest goal, the first priority, the source, the hiding place and the highest joy. 'Hallowed be your name!'

THE ROOT OF THE PROBLEM

In his letter to the Christian community in Rome, Paul sets forth the key messages of the gospel that he preaches. A significant concern is that, only a few years after the resurrection of Jesus, preachers stamped their very different impressions, each with a different emphasis, throughout the neighbouring countries.

The letter to the Romans is a milestone in the development of early church doctrine. To this day, the theology developed therein has formed the foundation for the Christian confession. After introductory greetings, Paul begins this great treatise by pointing out a problem: the world as it is today is on a collision course with God. It is only a matter of time before the judgment of God is revealed from heaven, according to this dismal prognosis (Romans 1:18). Now for a diagnosis. What exactly is it that is wrong in the world? There are many possible answers which might be conceived. Paul, however, attributes the adverse situation of humanity to just a single problem. What might that be? Is it the unfair distribution of goods? Is it a lack of education or enlightenment that holds people captive? Is it envy, egoism, or is it a lack of love? Maybe man's attachment to material things? All these answers have been, or will be, given by today's religious leaders, spiritual teachers and philosophers. None of these is Paul's answer. In fact, the real problem, the one that Paul identifies, is something that goes deeper than the 'sins' of humanity. It's about something which is at the foundation of sin, forming its root. Romans 1:19–21a says:

> *Since what may be known about God is plain to them, because God has made it plain to them. For since the creation of the world God's invisible qualities – his eternal power and divine nature – have been clearly seen, being understood from what has been made, so that people are without excuse.*
>
> *For although they knew God, they neither glorified him as God nor gave thanks to him*

While the Jewish people may have bypassed the law of God, according to Paul's argument, even the heathen are affected by the same God-problem.

Although they have the ability to discern God in the works of creation, people have not glorified and thanked God (Romans 1:21b). Is this, then, supposed to be the cause of the problem? According to Paul, yes.

In fact, on closer inspection, it shows how absurd it really is when the created one forgets the Creator, and fails to even give thanks. Paul says, 'Their thinking became futile and their foolish hearts were darkened. Although they claimed to be wise, they became fools'. (Romans 1:21b–22) There we have it again: the person who does not give thanks is foolish. Far from the beginning of wisdom, but rather, in the depths of delusion. Instead of fearing God, forgetting God.

Yet, the human dilemma persists. Instead of worshipping God, Paul continues, something else happened: '[They] exchanged the glory of the immortal God for images made to look like a mortal human being and birds and animals and reptiles'. (Romans 1:23) Anyone who has ever been to a museum of antiquities will not find it hard to imagine exactly what Paul was thinking. The Graeco-Roman world was full of statues of gods that they would burn incense to, and in the later stages of the Roman Empire it would become fashionable to import exotic idols of foreign peoples and serve those cults in a number of different ways.

The heart and the root of what he means, however, is not the question of what exactly was being prayed here. It is about the fact that 'the glory of God has been exchanged', that something else has taken the place of what really belongs only to the Creator.

Interestingly, all subsequent sin feeds on exactly that exchange.[71] Buried beneath all tangible, visible sins a problem seems to lie hidden deep in the heart of humankind. And it revolves around the question of who we worship.

What does it mean to worship something or someone? In the end it means to relate to what is most important to you. And it does not have to be an image of God or anything else religious. In concrete terms, there is something in every person's life that is of the utmost importance to them.

> So what do we trust and believe in? Have not money, power, reputation, public opinion, sex, become powers which the people bow to, and which gods they serve? [...] God is! – that means that there is sovereignty of truth and justice over all our purposes and interests.[72]

If you give credence to these words of Joseph Ratzinger, the urgent question is, then, not so much whether any person has

---

71 An ingenious analysis of Romans 1, which deepens this idea, can be found in: Raniero Cantalamessa, *Life in Christ: A Spiritual Commentary on the Letter to the Romans* (Liturgical Press, 2002).
72 Joseph Ratzinger, *The God of Jesus Christ: Meditations on the Triune God* (Ignatius Press, 2008).

done this or that sin, but what secret idols they serve, from the depths of their hearts? This is where the course of their life will be decided.[73]

This also explains why the topic of idolatry is omnipresent in the Bible. Is God so obsessed with his own authenticity that for him the demand for exclusive worship has such centrality? But the question of worship is so much more.

IDOLS OF THE HEART

The question of worship is one that is played out in the life of every human being: for whom and for what, ultimately, do you live? In the life of Jesus it is right at the beginning of his public work – where the Gospels present us with a gripping dialogue of the crucial confrontation between Jesus and the tempter.

> *Then Jesus was led by the Spirit into the wilderness to be tempted by the devil. After fasting for forty days and forty nights, he was hungry. The tempter came to him and said, 'If you are the Son of God, tell these stones to become bread.'*
>
> *Jesus answered, 'It is written: "Man shall not live on bread alone, but on every word that comes from the mouth of God."'*
>
> *Then the devil took him to the holy city and set him on the highest point of the temple. 'If you are the Son of God,' he said, 'throw yourself down. For it is written:*
> *"He will command his angels concerning you, and they will lift you up in their hands,*

73 Pope Benedict, speaking in a similar vein directly to the West during his visit to Bavaria in 2006 said: 'The peoples of Africa and Asia admire the technical achievements of the West and our science, but they are frightened by a kind of rationality that totally devours; God excluded from the field of vision of man, and consider this the highest kind of reason one also wants to teach their cultures. Not in the Christian faith do they see the actual threat to their identity, but in the contempt of God and in the cynicism, which regards the mockery of the saint as a right of freedom and benefit for the future success of the research to the last standard. Dear friend! This cynicism is not the kind of tolerance and cultural openness that the peoples are waiting for and we all want. The tolerance that we urgently need includes reverence for God – the reverence before what is sacred to the other. This reverence for the saint of others, in turn, presupposes that we ourselves should re-learn reverence for God. This awe can only be regenerated in the Western world when faith in God grows again – when God becomes present again for us and in us.' (Our translation.).

so that you will not strike your foot against a stone."'

Jesus answered him, 'It is also written: "Do not put the Lord your God to the test."'

Again, the devil took him to a very high mountain and showed him all the kingdoms of the world and their splendour. 'All this I will give you,' he said, 'if you will bow down and worship me.'

Jesus said to him, 'Away from me, Satan! For it is written: "Worship the Lord your God, and serve him only."'

MATTHEW 4:1–10

An interesting passage! It is preceded by the baptism of Jesus by John. After Jesus rises from the water, the sky opens and the voice of God speaks: 'This is my Son, whom I love; with him I am well pleased.' (Matthew 3:17b) Then, immediately afterwards, this identity is challenged. Show yourself as the true bearer of this title by turning stones into bread or falling from the top of the temple. Find confirmation in this, your divinity, by doing something great!

Yes, who wouldn't feel affirmed if they were able to produce such unequivocal evidence of their unique anointing by spectacular acts such as this? So why does Jesus reject the suggestion of the devil with such decisiveness? Would it really have been so wrong, for example, if he had turned a few stones into bread? It seems Jesus is going for something else. He does not respond to any of these suggestions. He simply refuses to heed any sentence that begins with 'If you are truly the Son of God'. Why? Because Jesus does not derive his identity from what he does, but rather from his relationship with the Father in heaven.

The foundational pattern of human life is one of performance orientation. We feel good, valued and affirmed when we are able to do something, when we are successful, when we have achieved something. This starts from the very earliest age: Daddy will be proud of me because I can ride my bike so well. What is understandable on the surface turns out to be less harmless when it becomes a pattern of life. When *doing* becomes more and more of a substitute for *being*. Someone who, even on their deathbed, is still thinking about what more they should have done in the office, has ultimately become a prisoner.

For more than a few, it takes a serious health crisis, exhaustion, depression or family failure to make them realize that they are no longer able to stop. That they have become driven. When the Bible talks about idolatry an interesting nuance arises:

> *Their land is full of idols;*
> *they bow down to the work of their hands,*
> *to what their fingers have made.*
> ISAIAH 2:8

> *That was the time they made an idol in the form of a calf.*
> *They brought sacrifices to it and revelled in what their*
> *own hands had made.*
> ACTS 7:41

In both passages it is emphasized that people are actually worshipping their own work in the form of idols. What they have made becomes god to them.

Why do people do what they do? Why does one strive for success in their career until their marriage lies in ruins; another nearly starve to death in an attempt to satisfy an arbitrary image of beauty, while a third is driven to pursue extreme sport to the point where their health collapses? Look back at Jesus' temptation in the desert. The devil offers him bread to eat, a spectacular flight down into a busy square in Jerusalem and, finally, immeasurable riches. Bread is about more than food. Jesus is close to starving. How consoling, how satisfying it must seem to him, the prospect of sinking his teeth into some fragrant, freshly-baked flatbread? This small convenience in this vast desert would at least be understood. It is ever thus with food: the tiny morsel of consolation, the crumb of comfort. After all, it is all about something concrete, survival: a little bread now would guarantee being able to get back. After forty days without food, no one is steady on their feet anymore. It's about his safety, his survival.

What is it about the leap off the highest point of the temple? Why the temple and not one of the steep cliffs of the Jordan valley? A leap from the highest wall of the temple right into the forecourt, filled with merchants and pilgrims: imagine the looks of amazement. Before the eyes of all men, Jesus would have been made known as a true Son of God and miracle worker. This temptation is that of recognition: which would then be assured.

The offer of 'all the riches in this world' is ultimately about power. Who would not be keen to rule over almighty Rome, the conqueror of all ancient kings, the rulers still wielding their sceptres in the misty barbarian forests north of the Alps, in the unexplored steppes of Nubia, high in the dangerous realm of the Parthians or even in the legendary mountainous countries of the Indus, up to which only Alexander the Great had been able to advance?

The three temptaions are all about power, recognition, comfort and security. And it is not by coincidence that these temptations, and just these, are chosen. These very four still constitute the idols of people's hearts. If you were to look carefully at your own heart, you yourself would soon realize how many actions are actually being fomented by these motives. The ability to influence and have something to say, to be among those who are in charge, is the ultimate motive of all possible human endeavour. And all that does happen in the world, is it not done with the hope of recognition? In the end, despite the number of good or bad deeds we do, is there no more motivation than the simple desire for an easier life, for a little more comfort and a consoling sticky plaster to mitigate for the hardships of life? And finally: the feeling of insecurity is scary for every human being, everyone has their strategies to build a secure framework.

In the fifth chapter of the Epistle to the Galatians, Paul lists behaviour patterns that result from a life 'in the flesh'. What is meant here is not so much a negative evaluation of the physical, rather there are sins with and without the participation of the body. These are fundamentally the hallmarks of a lifestyle that does not revolve around God but around one's own self:

> The acts of the flesh are obvious: sexual immorality, impurity and debauchery; idolatry and witchcraft; hatred, discord, jealousy, fits of rage, selfish ambition, dissensions, factions and envy; drunkenness, orgies, and the like. I warn you, as I did before, that those who live like this will not inherit the kingdom of God.
> GALATIANS 5:19–21

'Will not inherit the kingdom of God': any person who lets themselves be governed by these acts will not end up under the dominion of God, but somewhere else. It is not the good and life-giving authority of God that will guide him, but an idol, a false god.

If one thinks of Paul's argument at the beginning of the Epistle to the Romans, then one might conclude that behind every sin is an idol. And behind every idol is the fundamental lie that people can and must save themselves through their own efforts.

The four idols which are described in the temptation story are sometimes called 'idols of the heart'. These are the real force behind the behaviour that Paul calls 'works' and the effects of 'life in the flesh'. 'Sexual immorality' in the New Testament means sexual sin and includes any form of sexual activity outside of monogamous marriage between a man and a woman. In what ways can sexual sin be motivated by idols of the heart? The idol 'power' enjoys the idea of seducing and possessing anyone you can. 'Recognition' feeds on affirmation gained through a sense of one's sexual attractiveness. The idol 'comfort' promises relaxation and the alleviation of loneliness by infidelity, or a click on the pornography site. And how many unhealthy relationships feed on just that fear, that of losing all security if one were no longer to have a partner?

Paul also relates a whole list of interpersonal relationship issues to sin. How many disputes result from the desire to control another through physical violence, emotional blackmail, threats or greater intelligence? It's about power! If recognition is one's secret idol, being open to criticism and an honest request for forgiveness will hardly be possible. Those whose idol is comfort and consolation will value white lies, and will shy away from conflict at the cost of truth. And the desire for security can lead to controlling behaviour, to manipulation and defamation in order to join forces with another person and finally be safe from the evil outside world.

Paul also speaks of sins that are apparently religious in nature – idolatry and sorcery. Thus the practice of magic or ritual can be used as a mechanism of power. Moral supremacy, the certain knowledge of 'on the side of the good' and a self-righteous view of 'those unbelievers', turn out to be the religious forms of a pious dance before the idol of recognition. Religious accomplishments can promise comfort and are particularly convenient where they do not require a change of heart. And finally, any kind of devout practice can become a haven of security and self-affirmation: the constant danger of institutionalized religion creeping in and serving as a substitute for the daily fresh adventure of faith.

And finally, the material and physical sins that Paul refers to have their roots in something else: envy and factions arise where people and relationships are measured only in terms of their material benefits for the expansion of one's own sphere of financial power. And how much of the search for money and luxury is nothing more than a desperate search for recognition. The insatiable greed for emotional comfort and consolation is the mother of our physical addictions. We surround ourselves with material wealth or an abundance of food and alcohol, so that life is much less threatening.

It is a performance-based lifestyle that we absorb with our mother's milk and to which we are trained in this world. It holds us captive because it makes empty promises of fulfilment through power, recognition, comfort and security. The decision is forced upon us, becoming increasingly inexorable with every minute:

> 'No one can serve two masters. Either you will hate the one and love the other, or you will be devoted to the one and despise the other. You cannot serve both God and Money.'
> MATTHEW 6:24

●•.•°•.•°● ●.•°•.•°•.

EXODUS FROM SLAVERY

'Yahweh alone is God' – the shout of every voice raised after the spectacular showdown between Elijah and the four hundred priests of Baal on Mount Carmel (1 Kings 18:39). The statement that 'only God alone is God' sounds like a pleonasm[74] at first. Of course, only God is God, just like an apple is an apple. But something deeper is meant here. This statement implies that all other powers only claim to be God. They fail to fulfil their promise. Likewise, the four idols of the heart. They promise to fulfil the deepest of human needs; something without which a person can't know who they are. What would a human being be without any power, without any influence, scorned by all, without consolation and without any security? They would be a nobody. When you have something, that's what you are. And if you have nothing, you are nothing.

In the entire Bible, few statements are as central as the statement that God liberates his people. 'With a mighty hand the LORD brought us out of Egypt, out of the land of slavery.' (Exodus 13:14b) So goes the confession of Israel, repeated every year – even today at the *Seder*, or Passover meal. When God encounters the Israelites they are in a position of servitude. They

---

74 A pleonasm is using additional but totally unnecessary words in a sentence e.g.; 'warning hot coffee is hot'.

serve another, the Egyptian Pharaoh; the people of Israel have a merciless slave driver who doubles their workload and knows no mercy. God's act of liberation is not just a humanitarian undertaking; there is another, more existential purpose. 'So that they may worship me in the wilderness' (Exodus 7:16) is God's message to the ruler of Egypt, as indicated earlier. God frees his children from the rule of a lawless despot to lead them back to worship him.

The problem with idols of the heart is that they dominate us. There is nothing wrong with favouring material wealth over poverty. On the contrary, the ability to make choices or live in safety are fundamental human needs. To deny these to anyone is to treat them as less than human. Who can live without recognition? So this can't be about God not wanting to grant people power, recognition, comfort and security. It's about good things that turn into idols when they become ends in themselves. The call to worship God alone as God becomes more significant when put into the context of the very real demands we find ourselves subject to in the course of everyday life. And mere lip service will not get you very far here:

> One can confess Christ with the mouth and deny his rule in practical life. Do we have an Image, a sense of how feeble, unreal, even almost unbelievable the Lordship of Christ is actually revealed through us Christians in comparison to the claims of power by the 'Lord of this world?' Honour, power, influence, art, science, technology, politics, money, pleasure, comfort. These are not only theoretically working concepts! They demand – once they become an idol – the goal in life, the highest sacrifices of their followers and worshippers.[75]

Idols of the heart are demanding. And they threaten to remove their favour if we act against them. A demotion in my profession would be the most terrible thing imaginable if my

75 Hans Bürki, *Im Leben Herrschen* (Wuppertal, 1960), p.13.

career is the idol to which I have sworn obedience. If my idol
is the pursuit of recognition, then a loss of social status due to
the embarrassment over some trickery or a few dubious little
games in the past coming to light, will seem like hell. Once I
start to serve the idol of my own perfect appearance, its grip
on my own heart becomes more and more merciless. For when
is beautiful 'beautiful enough'? And when is a goal in fitness
or weight loss ever fully accomplished? When is success and
a sense of power so great that you cease feeling powerless
and insignificant compared with others? When will I feel safe
enough? How many life insurance policies, security locks and
separate bank accounts will make me feel really safe? And
this longing for comfort within, can it ever be permanently
controlled, as I indulge in alcohol, films, sex, food and 'fun'?

Every idol demands sacrifice. And every idol calls for
punishment. Every idol finally promises a satisfaction that
never occurs. Like the famous donkey in *Winnie the Pooh*,
persuaded to constantly keep walking by means of a carrot
dangling from a stick, this idolatry holds everyone who does
not make a complete break from it. It is a feature of an idol that
it never forgives. An act of professional misconduct cannot be
absolved in a lifetime, if, for that person, their career is their
ultimate goal. And the believer whose religious practice, on
which their self-image relies, is based on recognition, will not
be able to forgive their own religious failure.

The idol eventually crosses a boundary and will no longer
be satisfied with external offerings. It wants the heart, and it
wants it completely. Sooner or later every idol will demand you
do something that actually contradicts your own conscience.
At this stage, idolatry has become so entrenched that it feels as
if it would be impossible to break free. Pure lies! At any point
Jesus invites us to join with him. Quite open in his temptations
now, it becomes clear that the invitation of the devil is to stand
outside the will of God. And quite openly now, Jesus' response
reveals what the Exodus can look like.[76]

---

76 Essential suggestions for this chapter are drawn from a highly readable, practical study on biblical coaching: Scott Thomas and Tom Wood, *Gospel Coach* (Zondervan, 2012).

•.•••.•••● ●.•••.•••.

WHO YOU ARE AND WHO I AM

'Did God really say ...?' Was the sentence with which the serpent set in motion the process of doubt in Adam and Eve. Does this God exist, really? Is he good, really? Can I trust that he knows what I need? Or do I have to find all that I need in life – power, recognition, comfort and security – myself, through my own efforts? A foundational question that lies within the hiddenmost part of the heart of every human being. Jesus calls the devil 'father of lies' (John 8:44), as that is the name of his very effective strategy. The basis of every form of idolatry is performance orientation. And the basis of performance orientation is a lie about people. This lie about people is founded on lies about God. Because, in the final analysis, the question of who God is and what he is like decides everything.

One step at a time. The consequence of the Fall, as related in the garden of Eden narrative, is the emergence of human shame. In fact, it is an anthropologically remarkable fact that, of all living creatures, man alone has come to the conclusion that he should wear clothing. That their eyes would be opened if they were to act against God's commandment, was what the serpent had promised Eve. Their eyes actually were opened, and then they realized that they were naked. Could this fact have escaped them before this? Apparently it was previously not a problem: they were not ashamed in front of one another (Genesis 2:25). What happened after the Fall was not that they suddenly became naked. Rather, that nakedness suddenly became something that seemed bad. That shame had entered their lives and now they had to do something so as not to feel naked anymore. It was a bizarre undertaking, to try to hide from an omniscient God in the garden, but somehow humanity had realized that something in them was not right. This awareness of their shame combines with their doubts about the goodness of God, with which the serpent had infected them. God was suddenly no longer the loving Creator, to whom humanity owed everything, but one from whom one had to hide (and could!); one who was not to be trusted and who obviously was not gracious enough to forgive a failing, even if one had just confessed it to him. And beneath performance orientation lies the deep life-lie, that man must, and is able to, do something to 'repair himself'. This life-lie is in league with lies about God. All these lies say that God is 'not enough'. It is precisely these lies that Jesus confronts with reference to Scripture: God alone nourishes me, God alone can be worshipped and he deserves obedience without being put to the test. God alone!

Jesus' refusal to 'prove' his 'sonship' stems from his rejection of these lies about God. He does not have to prove the assertion 'if you are the Son of God'. He is the Son of God and holds fast to it. Son. A man cannot *do* this, a man cannot *do* son. A son, that's something you are. Jesus receives the confirmation of the Father, completely free, and even before he has performed any miracles or great things in public. Beloved Son of the Father on which his pleasure rests! And that is why, throughout his life, Jesus will never have to serve an idol. He does not crave recognition, because he does 'not receive glory from people' (John 5:41 ESV) but only from the Father. Jesus does not have to hold on to power, indeed, he can even humble himself as a servant washing people's feet, because:

> Jesus knew that the Father had put all things under his power, and that he had come from God and was returning to God; so he got up from the meal, took off his outer clothing, and wrapped a towel round his waist.
> JOHN 13:3–4

He knows that God is Father. That he is good. And this makes him independent and undaunted, even before the Roman governor who sentences him to be executed.

And the unbelievable happens. This Jesus does not keep his relationship with God as Father to himself. He offers to reconcile every person who believes in him with God. And it's more than just reconciling: it is a place in his own family. To be allowed to call God as none but he himself may call him: Abba, Father, Dad.

The foundation of idolatry is a lie about humankind and lies about God. And the foundation of the liberation story of the Exodus is the truth that Jesus has revealed again: God is a Father. And through Christ we become his beloved children. And the night before his death, Jesus prays that we may all know that the Father loves us 'even as you have loved me'. (John 17:23c) How much does God the Father love his perfect Son Jesus? It is with this greatest love of the universe that everyone who places their trust entirely in Jesus can know they are loved by God.

And so it is the truth of the untamed God who frees people from slavery. If God is almighty, then my own power is not of paramount importance. When it is ultimately about his rule, then I can learn to respond with greater composure when my own sphere of influence is threatened. Then I do not have to cling to power anymore. If God is merciful, then I may release myself from the strict demands of a life in search of attention and affirmation. Criticism and my own failures will not kill me. Envy of others, vanity, and the constant urge to be at the centre of things, can be healed at its root when I realize that God is indeed merciful with my imperfections. If God is good, then my compulsive search for comfort, peace and enjoyment can cease. Then I'm allowed to enjoy things without having to be addicted. And if God is finally all powerful, then my safety and control are no longer my greatest needs. I can be flexible and a little patient, admit weaknesses and no longer have to have control of everything. Even submission is still an act of the greatest freedom, because we commit ourselves in free will. The symbol is the kneeling down: we do not kneel in front of other people and if we do, it is to express the importance of the other at this moment, such as in a marriage proposal. This person is then *holy* to me at that moment, as previously described. But kneeling down as an existential act only before God is a gesture of freedom. Just as Romano Guardini says:

> *Therefore let not the bending of our knees be hurried gesture, an empty form. Put meaning into it. To kneel in the soul's intention, is to bow down before God in deepest reverence ... let your whole attitude say, Thou art the great God.*[77]

And yes, that's exactly the truth about God: he is glorious, he is merciful, he is good and he is all powerful. It is precisely these truths about God that heal the human heart. It is precisely this Father who Jesus came to reveal and to whom he has opened a way.

The God of Jesus Christ is the biblical God. And that always means: the whole Bible. This God with all his bright and dark aspects, familiar and strange facets: this is the true God. And the whole of the Scripture testifies of him, not just a few selectively picked out stories:

> *All your words are true;*
> *all your righteous laws are eternal.*
> PSALM 119:160

And to worship him, to put him first, is the only thing that makes man's heart free and fulfilled. Deeper than any power, recognition, comfort and security this world has ever offered!

---

77 Romano Guardini, *Sacred Signs* (Pio Decimo Press, 1956), p.20.

BEFORE SUNRISE

I just need to pick something up before I get on the plane. Who voluntarily takes a flight at seven in the morning? The ice-cold wind cuts through my thin coat. Why does early March feel so wintery? It's still dark outside. I'll just go to the prayer room for a few moments while I'm here. This is the Prayer House in Augsburg, in the aforementioned renovated fitness centre in the district of Göggingen. My glasses fog up as I enter the warm room on the first floor. There is space for a good eighty people – somehow you sense that someone has been here before you. To pray. Yes, for the last few hours, people have been praying here. For the last thirty-five thousand hours.[78] Because the worship of God has not ceased in here for over four years. If you stay for a long time in a place like this, you forget how crazy it is. It started many years ago with the vision, the idea and the desire to have a place where people pray, day and night. In a style that makes it easy for youngsters and not very religious people to connect. And here she sits at the front of the prayer room with her guitar. Janina is one of our prayer house missionaries. One of about twenty young people who have completed their education or left their professions to lead a life of prayer. A vocation in which they depend on providence – that is, on donations – that involves twenty-five hours of prayer a week, day and night.

As always, when I come to the prayer room at night – which admittedly is not often the case – it takes me a few minutes to realize what's happening here. I find the room shared by maybe eight pray-ers. Almost all young adults, and that at 4.38 in the morning. A few hours later, it will be certainly more. And so it continues: there is prayer 365 days a year and 24 hours a day, without a break.

So Janina sits here with her guitar and sings. Keeping her eyes fixed on the cross hanging at the front of the prayer room. In the middle of the night, there is hardly anyone there. Who

78 We have now been praying for far more than 35,000 hours. For up-to-date information on this, prayer missionaries and the work of the Augsburg Gebetshaus see gebetshaus.org.

is she singing for? She sings for God; she would still sing if no one else was there. Here she sits, having taken on this radical lifestyle. 'Does God require this?' Is this some kind of religious performance sport?

I listen to what she is singing. Or what others, dozens, hundreds of worshippers a week will pray and sing. 'You are worthy of it all', is one of the songs that is played here especially often, or, 'We love your name and we will not stop singing', is the chorus of a song that originated here in the house of prayer. Worship by day and by night, for one simple reason: because God is worthy to be worshipped for his own sake.

If I ask Johannes, who previously went through combat training for an elite unit of the German Army, why he now leads the night shift in the prayer house and gets up, night after night, to pray for four hours, with his intense eyes and robust male laugh, he will say the same thing. It is mostly young people who keep the prayer going. And there are more and more. The annual conference of the prayer house, *MEHR*, has grown rapidly in recent years, from 140 to 5,000 participants. Tens of thousands more on the Web-stream, on the Internet, on Christian television. What awaits you there and what awaits you in the house of prayer itself?

Quite simply, a fascination with a God so wonderful, so glorious and so powerful that it is the most natural reaction in the world to worship him, day and night. In passionate praise, in bold acts of faith, which are sometimes costly. Some prayer house missionaries have had to leave well-paid and secure jobs to live with the risks of living by faith and living a life of worship. And so I sit here yawning and can hardly believe it myself. The hours before dawn. I have to go soon. Life goes on and my plane will not wait. But as it has so often before, it cuts deep into my heart. These worshippers are out of this world. These crazy ones. They have stepped off the treadmill, left the circus. They live differently.

An hour later I am at the departure gate. The BOSS shop window displays the current spring collection. It will display another collection next year. Opposite, the perfect make-up palette. I head towards the new sports car from McLaren, now sitting, low and orange, incarnate before me to be admired. Now to the sushi bar – or to perfumes in the duty-free? I make my way through a horde of suits, all very busy. Everyone checking their mobile phones. *Financial Times* or *Telegraph,* business or economy class, Dubai, Taipei or Chicago, milk and sugar in your coffee? 'Welcome aboard!' I'm sitting in my window seat when the full force of the situation comes to mind again. 'In the unlikely event of sudden pressure loss, oxygen masks will automatically fall from above.' I do not take in the safety instructions. Outside, the darkness has given way to a blue-grey canvas, which becomes gently brighter towards the bottom, with an orange strip at the end. Early fog hangs like cotton wool tufts in the hollows on the edge of the forest. A red light flashes on the wing.

Here I am sitting on a plane and the world keeps rushing on in this race. Why is that? Boarding is complete, a tanker curves past. All at once, it seems to me that what I had experienced earlier in the prayer room was not at all like anything crazy. It seems the most normal thing in the world to me. And I am so thankful that someone is praying right now. That the morning shift took over at six, as on all other 365 days of the year. And that there are a few people of wisdom in this vortex of nothingness and dizziness. In this carousel, where I live too. Those who fear God. Who watch for him at night. And wait for the sunrise.

I am pushed back into the grey leather of the seat. The plane has taken off, leaving the fog banks far below. A peaceful landscape is now below me. Finally, the sun breaks through from behind the Alps and illuminates the peaks in brown light. A bright red balloon of glistening rays. Up here, the sky is always blue, and up here, the sun always shines. My plane is flying to London, but my heart stays behind with my crazy friends in Augsburg. I have to think about them now. My friends with this wise lifestyle. And I know that one day the sun will rise. Then it will be the worshippers who go before the rising of the sun. The night does not last forever. The day comes as surely as the tide after the ebb. And in the light, it all becomes visible, what really counts, and what, like sand, is sifted away.

• • • • • • • • • ● ●•• • • • • •

OUT OF THE COMFORT ZONE!

It's time to break out. A personal exodus is coming. And also, finally, an exodus for the church here in the West. If she wants to remain, or rather, become, believable and powerful again, something fundamental will have to change. And this something will have to involve the fear of God, and worship.

Throughout history, God has called men and women to make a difference. In the history of Israel there were so-called 'judges' who were chosen by God to bring salvation to the people, even before the birth of the kingdom of Israel. Gideon was one of the first of these judges. Something interesting is said about him. In fear of the enemy Midianites who plundered the Israelites, Gideon threshes wheat in a winepress. The future hero of the people, therefore, seems to be as timid a man as everyone else. No wonder, then, that he doesn't make much of the greeting of the angel, 'The LORD is with you, mighty warrior.' (Judges 6:12) Gideon is as discouraged as all the others. Nevertheless, God calls him to fight against the occupiers and to restore freedom to his nation.

But before this can happen, a first step is required. The next night God himself speaks to Gideon and instructs him:

> 'Take the second bull from your father's herd, the one seven years old. Tear down your father's altar to Baal and cut down the Asherah pole beside it.'
> JUDGES 6:25

Why must Gideon seize his father's possessions? In the ancient Middle Eastern world, families were close communities of providence. What applies to the whole family affects the life of the individual family member deeply. So the father's altar to Baal is not just any object; it is the family idol. Only when Gideon breaks with these idols does he receive the power to lead the whole people to freedom.

True transformation – of a person, a whole church or a whole society – always begins directly in the life of the individual. Before one can turn to generally unjust circumstances, the question of one's own heart will always arise. The question of one's own idolatry. Here, exactly here, is where the exodus begins. It's easy to get upset with other people or complain about a flawed structure. But with great insight into human nature, the book of Proverbs admonishes us:

> *Do not let your heart envy sinners,*
> *but always be zealous for the fear of the LORD.*
> PROVERBS 23:17

Do you yourself strive to have no Asherah poles, no idolatry, in your life? Then reach out, in fear of God. That, precisely, is a departure out of the spiritual comfort zone. This farewell, if it is fully accomplished, is always a break with the things we have come to love. A break almost always with what people around you find very normal. It is no coincidence that it is his family members whom Gideon must first stand up against in his new calling. It is in the family that people learn the true religion of the heart. Regardless of which creed children learn, they sense which values really count. What to be proud of. Who to look down on. Which rules are in no circumstance to be violated. And when to turn a blind eye.

Our own idols of the heart are often learned in the family. And everyone is under the slavery of sin. Therefore, the true worship of God and the fear of the Lord are not acquired in passing. It requires a clean cut, the decision to put God first. A decision that is only real when you feel it challenges your heart.

God alone is my safety and I reject my ways of self-protection. I choose to trust in God.

God alone deserves honour and I reject my urge for validity. I choose to find my greatness through honouring the Lord of Lords.

God alone is good and I deny my self-seeking search for consolation and comfort. I choose to accept God's good gifts for me.

God is merciful and loves without condition. That's why I reject my addiction to recognition. I choose to live more under the eye of God than under the eye of people.

A PRAYER BY THE AUTHOR

This small prayer should not be spoken lightly. It contains a completely revolutionized life plan. And it starts with the first step: the decision. The cutting down of the cult totem pole: this far and no further! I'm breaking out! The second step, however, is equally important. Life without God at the centre is a deeply flawed life. A life that misses the target. This is more than a question of style. The decision to break out of the religious comfort zone does not become real without genuine repentance. Christian repentance does not include any form of self-punishment – you will have to pay for that! – but deep personal sorrow. There is no true repentance without sorrow. Mourning for having received everything from the Creator, but not having given back to him what is, unquestionably, his. A grief that is not hopelessly introspective, but exactly the opposite. It is just a turning away from circling around oneself.

In a serious marriage crisis, someone who recognizes – with true contrition – how much they have hurt and misunderstood their partner does well to face this pain. This is necessary for true transformation. Anyone who has lived a lifetime with false gods on the throne of their heart, and who has paid little attention to the one true God, would be well advised to appreciate the full weight of missing this target. It is a salutary pain; it is the sting the eye feels when it suddenly looks into the sun after far too long in the dark. Such is the process of repentance, which gains substance if we do not do it on our own. The Catholic understanding of the sacrament of reconciliation has gone a little out of fashion. No wonder: today's narcissistic society perceives talk of personal sin as offensive. And yet exactly therein lies liberation: I stand by my faults. I do not have to hide them, because I know that God is merciful. Maybe it would be good to confess once again. And then not to confess any single sin, but to go to the root of the problem. The idols of the heart. On a trivialization of God. And then the second chapter of the book of Proverbs gives an answer to the question of how the fear of God can grow:

> *My son, if you accept my words*
> > *and store up my commands within you,*
> *turning your ear to wisdom*
> > *and applying your heart to understanding –*
> *indeed, if you call out for insight*
> > *and cry aloud for understanding,*
> *and if you look for it as for silver*
> > *and search for it as for hidden treasure,*
> *then you will understand the fear of the* LORD
> > *and find the knowledge of God.*
>
> PROVERBS 2:1–5

Our escape from our comfort zone, our existential exodus, involves practical steps that we derive from the word of God. A first step is that we unequivocally 'call out for insight' and 'cry aloud for understanding' in order to attain an attitude of the fear of God. For after the new decision for a God centred life and with deep repentance, a new priority needs to replace the old one. Aquinas teaches: 'The ultimate felicity consists in the contemplation of God'.[79] And now it's time to continue on our way. If you renounce your idols of the heart, you may be tempted to question whether you will come up short, if from now on you no longer seek to be powerful, recognized,

---

79 Thomas Aquinas, *Summa contra Gentiles* III 37.

comforted and secure. One of the most enlightening things about human happiness comes from an author who can say he has learned the essence of life in a place where happiness is more remote than anywhere else: as a young man Victor Frankl experienced the horrors of the concentration camp. Even in this environment of utter despair, he realized that there were people who could not be broken. His theory, later developed under the name *Logotherapy*, says that man finds himself only when he finds meaning. However, meaning is not only found in 'fulfilling oneself'. In a small interview that I found only on the Internet, Frankl compares people with an eye.[80] A healthy eye is characterized by the fact that it does not see itself. Anyone who constantly perceives a greenish patch in his field of vision has impaired eyesight. The eye is still fully functional when the person does not perceive the actual eye, but instead the trees, the sun and the sea.

Frankl uses this comparison to reject the claim that man finds himself looking at himself and his needs. It is precisely man's surrender to something greater – what Frankl calls 'self-transcendence' – that brings him fulfilment, brings him meaning. Theologically interpreted, this means that man is not created for himself. He is the creature of a glorious God, who created him as a free counterpart to his beauty and his love. He is the only creature created for his own sake, and therefore finds fulfilment only in the surrender of himself to the Creator, as the fathers of the Second Vatican Council have formulated so impressively.[81]

Another step in the personal exodus is to turn to God in prayer. Ask for insight and enter into dialogue with God. A Christian life is not possible without prayer. What does not actually take place in time and space may instead be a pious feeling or platonic desire. But a relationship with God becomes real when definite times of the day and week are devoted exclusively to prayer. It's not surprising that learning a foreign language or

80 https://youtu.be/F7GwzAJPARg (13.10.15).
81 Gaudium et Spes 24,3.

doing weekly fitness training actually requires practice and repetitive routine. Nobody would expect to become athletic or lose weight by reading a book about it and finally being convinced. A definite change of life begins with definite behavioural changes. So, take this step: take time for personal prayer regularly, preferably daily. How long this time is exactly is not crucial. More important is that it actually takes place, as we are creatures of habit. However, choose a period of time that is long enough to be able to quieten yourself. Two minutes will not be enough for that. For me, a day without an hour of prayer would be unimaginable. It's the same for my wife, who is the mother of four small children. One hour, does that seem like a lot of time? It is significantly less than the average time spent watching TV or on the Internet per day. But the question of what governs our hearts becomes visible in the question of the priorities of our routines. What do we hallow?

The next step, ultimately, is to do the looking for and searching that Proverbs speaks of. The suggestion is: get to know God! Get to know him where he reveals himself most clearly. And that is in the Holy Scriptures. One hint is important: the Bible is a collection of books that belong together. Through individual Bible verses, almost any and every nonsense can be ascertained. However, the Scriptures in totality draw a fascinating and complex picture of God. Do not be afraid: you do not have to be a theologian to understand the Bible. Start with the New Testament. Read two chapters a day and let the readings flow into your prayer – your dialogue with God. Anyone who reads four chapters a day can read the New Testament in a month. Anyone who reads for eighty hours – that's how long an average German spends watching TV in a month – has read the entire Bible at a normal reading speed. Once through the New Testament, start over again. And then you can dare to read the Old Testament. Read them in this order, because the Old Testament is only understandable in the light of Jesus Christ and his message in the New Testament. And whenever you come to a facet of God that alienates you or a place that you do not understand, then value it as a challenge. God is greater than our mind: he breaks our preconceived categories. Where you keep bringing your irritations, doubts and complaints to God, true adoration and true fear of the Lord will then start shaping your life more and more. The promises of such a life are astonishing:

> Fear of man will prove to be a snare,
>   but whoever trusts in the LORD is kept safe.
>
> PROVERBS 29:25

He who fears God no longer has to fear people. He who stands under the gaze of the Most High can also stand upright before men. And so too the book of Proverbs goes on with its outlook on what flourishes to those who fear God:

> For the LORD gives wisdom;
>   from his mouth come knowledge and understanding.
> He holds success in store for the upright,
>   he is a shield to those whose way of life is blameless,
> for he guards the course of the just
>   and protects the way of his faithful ones.
>
> Then you will understand what is right and just
>   and fair – every good path.
> For wisdom will enter your heart,
>   and knowledge will be pleasant to your soul.
> Discretion will protect you,
>   and understanding will guard you.
>
> Wisdom will save you from the ways of wicked men,
>   from men whose words are perverse,
> who have left the straight paths
>   to walk in dark ways,
> who delight in doing wrong
>   and rejoice in the perverseness of evil,
> whose paths are crooked
>   and who are devious in their ways.

Wisdom will save you also from the adulterous woman,
  from the wayward woman with her seductive words,
who has left the partner of her youth
  and ignored the covenant she made before God.
PROVERBS 2:6–17

It is like having a compass in the heart of those for whom God comes first. A feeling for a good life and a deep fulfilment within it. A reluctance to go down slippery paths. Restraint in calling things right that everyone else calls right. A protection from harm, and an understanding of true perspectives. Actually, almost all aspects of life seem to be addressed. As if everything would fall into the right perspective if people let God be God. To fear him, to take him to the centre. That is the message of Christianity: that everything revolves around this God. And our relationship with him decides everything. This majestic God, this eternal, holy God. The God who transcends our categories with his holiness, his untamed nature.

Bursting glass. With a fearful look at the thin glass in the windows and a bottle of cheap Retsinas, this gruesome day comes to an end. It had started long before dawn. We had risen prayerfully at dawn. Down there on the stone floor in front of the now-extinguished fireplace in the guest house of Agia Anna. In the guesthouse of the monastic settlement on Athos, of which we had read so much. Especially in Archimandrite Cherubim's report; Tom had brought it from some Orthodox monastery and given it to me. A book in pale yellow paper with the peculiar title *From the Garden of Panagia*, memories of the sacred Mount Athos. In it the author reports on a few monks, most of whom led a life of renunciation and prayer in the nineteenth century. Up amongst the fissured cliffs of the southern peaks on the Athos peninsula. The zeal for God has something contagious. And indeed, it had been our desire to do the same as those friends of God that led us to gently descend the creaking wooden staircase, well wrapped up in the depth of the night, to pray to God before the sun rises. For hours, the black beads of the Greek prayer rope glide through our fingers to the sound of the Jesus Prayer. There is something extraordinary about praying in this place, in which there has been prayer for centuries. To this place where those men lived a holy life of which we had read about in the memories *From the Garden of Panagia* (*the most holy* referring to Mary, the mother of Jesus). I did not know then that it would be my last stay on Athos with Tom. I did not know yet that one day I would look back on those anxious hours before a stormy day as the last hours of prayer together on the holy mountain. But I still see us standing there in the pale light of the departing night with the wind howling. Two young men looking for God. Two friends.

Agia Anna is a collection of loosely scattered hermitages within the area, with their domes, balconies and gardens. If you come from the summit of Mount Athos, after a fork in the road, a view suddenly opens up of the unimaginable vastness of the sea. A sea that glistens 700 metres below. You have to descend a short distance through the shady foliage of the oaks and plane trees until you come to the forecourt of the Agia Anna church. From here too: all around nothing but the sea. Turning one's gaze, one sees that the monastic settlement extends to the whole semicircle of the steep valley, which slopes down to the shore. There are cottages above, majestically clinging to the craggy rock, peering directly out of the side of the forest, perched higher up on a hilltop. And in the midst: you yourself, as if in an orchestra pit, surrounded by silent ranks. It is exactly this image that Archimandrite Cherubim handed down from one of the former inhabitants of Agia Anna. He lived like the Apostle Paul, who said that his life as an apostle is like a spectacle staged by God, so that angels and men alike can read of his life, and what it means to follow Christ (see 1 Corinthians 4:9). He felt the life in this settlement's semi-circular valley was like a fight in the amphitheatre. Not in the eyes of people, but under the gaze of God and the monks who before him had lived, suffered and loved here.

Life as a fight, life as a spectacle, life as something that counts. Even the most hidden acts count, a heroism of everyday decisions. It was our last stay on Athos. This night, in which we feel like competitors in the arena, who live for an eternal reward, for the Eternal.

Maybe youthful eccentricity, and yet the last of our trips to this place. A few years later and Tom is now dead and I'm still alive. It was on one of the tear-soaked days in August when I accidentally clicked on Tom's profile that was still on our homepage, along with his photo. Each of us had such a profile and there, in addition to age, marital status and responsibilities, in a few words he described what his life's dream was. All kinds of things were there. In my file, something about big plans and important projects. Tom was already dead when I first read what he had written there years earlier. And literally it says, 'To love Jesus every day, more than yesterday, and at the end of my life, to have walked in the works God prepared for me, to have run the good race.' (Ephesians 2:10)

It was the travelling and nights like those stormy ones that called forth something in my friend to a deep, heartfelt truth: that in the end it was only about HIM. To run the good race: it is Paul's metaphor and of the amphitheatre, a life about the highest price of victory. Exactly the imagery of the hidden fights in the arena of Agia Anna. It was not long before I rewrote my staff profile. It was still during the midsummer weeks of pain that I went deeper and deeper into myself: what do you live for? Which prize are you running for?

The glass will burst. The storm will come. No window can withstand it anymore. And every road I take flows inevitably down to the coast. Every country borders the boundless ocean. For how much longer will we run from it? I am no longer on the mainland, but in the boat, the world is an island and nothing more. For me, one has sailed on ahead. The one who knows what kind of reality he has to deal with will become a little more circumspect. We will no longer be afraid of some things but more afraid of others. But he will fear and love God, just like the sea. Be content with the fact that God is infinite, that he is wild like the rough sea. Terrifyingly wonderful like the ocean. And terrifyingly beautiful. All categories and preconceived ideas being blown well apart. Untamed.